THE ABCs OF
DECORATING

THE ABCs OF DECORATING

Genevieve Fernandez

DOUBLEDAY & COMPANY, INC.
Garden City, New York

Library of Congress Cataloging in Publication Data

Fernandez, Genevieve.
ABCs of decorating.

Includes index.
1. Interior decoration.   I. Title.
NK2110.F47   1982   747.213
AACR2
ISBN 0-385-18511-1
Library of Congress Catalog Card Number 80–2448

Design by Jeanette Portelli
9 8 7 6 5 4

*To the Memory of
My Husband, Bill*

❦ Contents ❧

❧ Introduction ❧

The art of decorating the home is just that—an art, a learned craft, a honed technique. It's a skill that the professional masters only after years of study and practical experience, an expertise that you, the untrained amateur, must somehow grasp in enough time to create a pleasing and harmonious decor for your own home. How can this be accomplished? By learning the ABCs of decorating—the basics—and understanding how to put them into practice. By digesting the fundamentals, observing the guidelines, and coming to terms in as honest and realistic a way as possible with your deepest feeling about comfort, color, and design. This book will give you those fundamentals, and will guide you, step by step, along the challenging and sometimes complicated route of home decoration, explaining the problems and the pitfalls, the do's and the don'ts, and the kind of analysis and planning that must be put into any interior design project if it is to succeed.

Not too long ago, a well-known American psychologist stated that decorating the home was one of the crisis points in a woman's life. An appreciative murmur ran through the audience, a group of professional women; the speaker was also a woman.

Today the scene is somewhat different. Men as well as women experience the traumas of decorating a home, whether it be a bachelor pad or a house that they share with wife, husband, friend, or family. Yet the crisis or trauma endures. Or is exacerbated, as the cost of furniture, fabrics, wallpapers, rugs, lighting designs, and accessories continues to escalate. Add to this the bewildering selection offered to us by home furnishings manufacturers—in style, material, pattern, and price. It is an embarrassment of riches that can confuse, even overwhelm, us.

Up to the point that we decorate our first home, our expenditures have been relatively small, and we have been purchasing items that we know and understand. And then one day we are faced with the prospect of spending sizable amounts of money on three or four empty rooms. Or redoing a home that had been "thrown together" as a makeshift arrangement. And somehow, without any understanding of what goes with what, of which piece to put where, of how to handle walls and windows or implement a color scheme, we are asked to spend this money wisely and well. We are expected to make intelligent choices from the superabundance of merchandise that is available to us, selecting what is right and rejecting what is wrong, and trusting that blind luck will help us create a beautiful and comfortable haven.

But we need so much more than mere blind luck. We need to understand how to go about it, where to start, what to choose, how to arrange it, light it, accessorize it. Once we know what we are doing and where we are going, the crisis of decorating becomes a challenge, a challenge that we can meet head on, with a sense of adventure and fun.

Some beginners, unfortunately, take a dim view of their own potential, discouraged by the so-called decorating mystique. This mystique, nurtured by a few professionals, assumes that design talent is innate, like blue eyes or freckles. You either have it or you don't. If asked to explain decorating technique, they might respond in a fashion similar to that of the late, lamented jazz musician Fats Waller when asked about the meaning of rhythm: "If you got to ask, you ain't got it."

Most of the very competent professional designers we know welcome participation by their clients, and strive to include many of their present possessions in the redecoration of their homes. They try to get their clients involved and interested in the procedure, for they know that out of this will come a home that blends their own expertise with the special personality and tastes of the family itself.

You want to create a home that is real, not one that has been perfectly "done." You will take lasting pleasure in rooms that offer comfort and convenience, not mere visual impact.

Often one may feel hampered by a real shortage of space, by the fact that the work needed to maintain a home is done by you and your family. But such limits can give focus and direction to the decorating. Furnishings are purchased and arranged with an eye toward opening up and redefining existing space. Materials are selected for their durability, ease of maintenance, and soil resistance, as well as for their aesthetic beauty. Such restrictions force a certain honesty upon the decorating approach, and the style of a home that emerges from such honesty is likely to be much more real and more personal.

From the minute we first opened our eyes, we have been learning about the world around us, about the colors, shapes, and textures furnished by man, nature, or machine. Each time we admire fresh flowers or fruits and vegetables in an open stall, walk into an art gallery, observe the neighborhood architecture, or visit a friend's home, we take stock of all the possibilities, we add to our visual frames of reference, we develop our own taste, we exercise a critical eye. And all that we assimilate comes to our aid once we begin a decorating project.

For getting started is the hardest part. And it's the part that often takes the most study and preparation. We don't just dive into our decorating adventure and hope for the best; we need to put extensive thought and time into developing the plan and making changes as we go along. And once we have established our basic decorating scheme, we invest just as much effort into carrying it out. If our preliminary work has been thorough, this part of the job will be relatively easy and will prove most enjoyable.

The purpose of this book is to provide you with a start-to-finish game plan on the ABCs of decorating. You will learn how to prepare yourself for the venture, how to appraise your needs, work up a budget, pick a starting point, develop a color sense.

Part I of the book will also give you a useful primer on the history of furniture design.

In Part II we discuss all the "tools of the trade," dealing with the principles of background decoration (walls, windows, floors), with the essentials of furniture selection and arrangement, storage needs, and lighting strategy.

We proceed logically to Part III, which centers on the specific design and living challenges relevant to each and every room of the house: living rooms, dining rooms, bedrooms, kitchens, bathrooms, children's rooms, hobby rooms, family rooms, hallways, and foyers.

We finish up, appropriately, in Part IV with a section on finishing touches. Here we discuss the "where" (tabletops, walls, cabinets, sofas, and shelves) and the "what" (accent designs, pillows, wall decor, quilts and afghans, collectibles) of accessorizing.

Working in natural progression, we show you how to proceed the way the professionals do—by building a portfolio for each room that is to be decorated. These portfolios will help you develop, work through, organize and expedite each of your decorating projects.

part one

THE ABCs OF GETTING STARTED

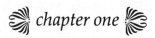 *chapter one*

Learn It Yourself

Since decorating is not an exact science, it is not nearly as complex or as sophisticated as many think it to be. The various mystiques that have evolved around interior design do not have lasting substance, and a new approach that sometimes receives great fanfare in the press is often nothing more than a simple solution to current spatial problems and living styles. It does not take extraordinary talent or great intellectual ability to become adept at what comes naturally to man: feathering his nest.

Bone Up on Furniture Design

A course in the history of the decorative arts is the first basic of any decorating course, whether you take it at an accredited school or one that you program for yourself. And you *can* program one for yourself. By observing the manner in which man furnished his houses and castles over the centuries, you can trace the development of furniture styles and understand the architectural trends and practical requirements that shaped them. The various ways in which home furnishings were designed and were used to cope with life inside the home, before the advent of central plumbing and heating, can also throw a great deal of light upon the understanding of the various periods of furniture design.

This program would include a number of trips to the library to borrow any good survey books on furniture design or to read whatever reference encyclopedias might be available on the world of decorative arts. This could be supplemented, at the same time, with trips to museums that have period displays and visits to local antique shops. If no museums of this kind are located near the town in which you live, you might consider making a weekend jaunt to a city where one exists. Many families build an entire vacation around a trip to a famous restoration, such as those in Williamsburg, Virginia; Wilmington, Delaware; Salem, Massachusetts; Newport, Rhode Island, and so on. These restorations, and many others found primarily in the eastern and southern areas of the United States, report a flourishing interest, to such an extent that "restoration hopping" can be considered a national pastime.

Another activity that is not only interesting but educational for the budding amateur decorator is auctions. Even if one does not attend the auction itself, a great deal is to be learned from viewing the items on display during the exhibition period that precedes each auction. It's worth the few dollars to invest in the auction catalog, as this often gives a full description, approximate date of manufacture, and estimated selling price for each piece to be auctioned off. If you make auction going a regular occurrence, you will be surprised at how quickly and easily you will absorb the pertinent facts about each design genre.

Many of the popular magazines that feature decorating projects produce special issues dedicated to Early American decorating, as studies show that it is still one of the most popular looks for today's home. Even if you do not intend to use this style in your own interiors, it makes sense to see the kind of furniture that was used two hundred years ago, and to grasp the special solutions that it offered. Lightly scaled American traditional upholstery and cabinet designs were a fitting answer to the smaller, low-ceilinged rooms of the early colonists. Since we face similar problems in today's builder-designed houses and apartments, it is not surprising that there has been a resurgence of interest in these Colonial designs, for they not only work beautifully in undersized rooms but add a special charm and character to lackluster architecture.

Steeping yourself in the history of decorative arts by studying reference books and definitive publications on interior design, as well as by visiting museums, restorations, and auction exhibits, will certainly begin to build up your frames of reference. It is also just as important to familiarize yourself with the contemporary world of home furnishings and interior design. This you can accomplish more easily by picking up newsstand copies of leading decorating and architectural magazines, by viewing model rooms at your local furniture and department stores and those in decorator showhouses, and by visiting stores and showrooms that specialize in fabrics, wallpapers, rugs, lighting fixtures, etc. By doing this, you will not only get a good idea of what is currently available and how much it costs, but also a sense of what you find pleasing and attractive. Almost unconsciously you will start the process of selection and rejection that is an integral part of any interior design project. Jot down a note or two about any room or home furnishings design you like and learn about what especially appeals to you.

How to Discover Your Own Design Taste

Review these preferences, and see what kind of pattern has emerged; it may be that you have zeroed in on one specific decorating mood— possibly country French or architectural modern. Or you may have collected a grand mix of style moods that cut across every period. In the first case, it will be easy for you to deduce which period look is for you; in the second instance, you will have discovered just what kind of mix or eclectic effect you admire and want for yourself.

While you have been going through the process of discovering your own personal design preferences, you should also be honing and improving your taste. You will begin to notice that a beautifully designed chair has grace, balance, symmetry, and is skillfully crafted of beautiful materials. An attractive interior styled with taste also has balance, grace, and charm, plus harmony—the marvelous synthesis of all the individual design elements—to create a whole that is indeed more wonderful than any one of its parts.

By viewing all that the home furnishings market produces, observing quality of design, material, and workmanship, you will be able to discern certain standards of taste, both in individual design elements and in the putting together of the whole room.

FASHON® WALLCOVERINGS BY GENERAL TIRE/GTR WALLCOVERING CO.

Unpredictable combinations, such as plastic-sheathed Parsons table with rush-seated French country chairs, give this dining area its special flair. Floor is paved with brick-look vinyl, while the brick motif is repeated in wall-covering pattern. Recessed alcoves are dramatized by a contrasting wall covering in a colorful plaid.

The Basics of Period and Style

So that you can tell the difference between one design period and another, so that you can clarify your own very personal taste preferences, we are giving, in the following paragraphs, our outline of the basic historical periods of designs and styles in the decorative arts starting with seventeenth-century designs and ending with contemporary. To simplify this very broad range, we will concentrate only on those periods that have had a broad, sweeping, and lasting influence on the evolution of the decorative arts as we know them today.

Seventeenth-Century Influences

The significant developments in furniture and interior design really began in the seventeenth century; most furniture before this time (unless one goes back to the early Romans and Greeks) was of the massive, dark, and somewhat crude styles that characterized much of what was used to fill the homes and castles of the Middle Ages and early Renaissance periods. A new interest in comfort, greater ornamentation and carving, as well as the development of new kinds of furniture such as the settee (the predecessor of the sofa) and the highboy (previously only low chests had been used for storage) mark the salient characteristics of this period. These developments took place concurrently in England and in Central Europe, and are best known under the catchall labels of Jacobean (1603–49), Restoration (1660–89) and William and Mary (1689–1702) in England, and Louis XIV (1643–1715) in France. Furniture of the early part of the century was more massive, a transitional link from earlier times. Large, paneled beds and two-part trundle styles were free-standing designs that replaced the built-in alcove beds of the previous periods. Chairs gained front legs and stretchers, these often boasting decorative turnings and carvings; chests squatted on ball feet or stood higher on taller legs and stretchers. Veneering was developed in the latter half of this century.

It is worth noting that comparable design developments took place in the New World, but the American versions were, of course, cruder and simpler in design and execution. Painted finishes, which emerged with the japanning (lacquer work) of Jacobean and William and Mary pieces as additional decoration, were employed to cover unattractive graining and flaws in the woods used for the more rustic Early American designs. Many of the classic gateleg and trestle tables that are still so popular today derived from this early period.

The French designs of the seventeenth century were, of course, more elegant, as they were geared to the life of the French court. Here we note the emergence of marble as a tabletop material, the use of gilding, ormolu, inlay, and lacquer. Upholstered benches, with elegantly carved frames and legs, were also noteworthy as a new development of this era in France.

Eighteenth Century—The Golden Age

The eighteenth century reigns supreme as the golden age of decorative arts; it was during this century of booming trade and commerce that the great cabinetmakers made their monumental contributions to the superb catalogs of English and French traditional furniture. More people could afford to live with greater comfort and style, and a whole new world of home furnishings was designed to meet their requirements.

Great craftsmen and designers, such as Thomas Chippendale, the Adam brothers, George Hepplewhite, and Thomas Sheraton would become legendary figures in the annals of eighteenth-century English furniture design, while in France, the great furniture contributions of the period would become world famous as the styles of the two reigning monarchs: Louis XV and Louis XVI. Adaptations of the classic English designs were gaining significance of their own in New England, notably among those cabinetmakers working in Newport, Rhode Island, and in Philadelphia, Pennsylvania.

The periods in England under which these cabinetmakers labored are known as the Queen Anne and Georgian eras, denoting the monarchs who held sway at the time. In the earlier part of the century, notably during the Queen Anne period, design developments included such features as the cabriole leg, ball and claw feet, shell ornamentation, dropleaf tables, chairs with splat back shaping, delicately scaled desks with batwing hardware, and the broken pediment top highboy. Chippendale, at first, continued the graceful curves of the Queen Anne period, using even more elaborately curved legs and ball and claw feet, but his later work reflects the influence of Chinese design, favoring square block legs, fretwork, ornate carving, and lacquer work, known as japanning. Later efforts by the Adams, Hepplewhite, and Sheraton reflect the

Queen Anne

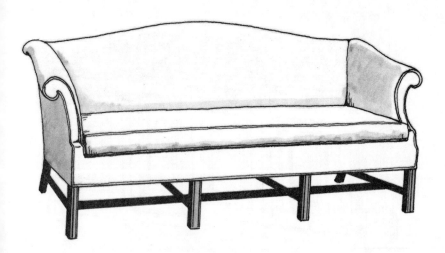

Chippendale Sofa

trend toward neoclassic shapes, inspired by the designs of antiquity. Adam designs are best recognized by their gracefully tapered legs, elegant oval-backed chairs and curved console cabinets, while Hepplewhite designs can be distinguished by such features as shield backs for chairs, fluting and reeding on legs, inlay, veneering, and painted motifs. Sheraton favored straight-lined furniture, as well as slender-tapered legs for chairs and tables, delicate proportions, and elegant detail carving.

Welsh Cabinet

Blockfront Chest

Shield-back Hepplewhite Chair

The French Interpretations

Furniture known as Louis XV can be most readily distinguished from the succeeding Louis XVI era by the shape of furniture legs—the earlier leg was curved, the later one straight.

During the Louis XV period, more than just the legs were curved; commodes were given bombé shaping, and the arms and backs of bergères and settees also featured a rounded form. Intricate carving and inlays, the lavish use of marble, marquetry, bronze doré ormolu, and caning were all rich and ornamental distinctions aimed to please the king and the nobility, and to adorn the lavish palaces and châteaus of the monarch and his court. This was also the era in which the superb Savonnerie carpets, marvelous damasks, brocades, and tapestries became commonplace in the interiors of the homes of French aristocrats.

The reign of Louis XVI parallels in design development the neoclassic aspects that characterized the cabinetry produced in England at the same time. Now legs were straight and fluted, cabinets were simplified and reflected the influence of Pompeii, whose great ruins were being excavated during this period.

Louis XVI Armchair

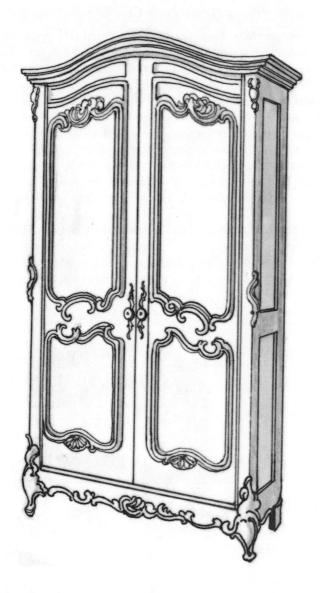

French Provincial Armoire

Classic Motifs of Nineteenth-Century Furniture

Nineteenth-century furniture design started off with the classic shapes and motifs that we associate with the Empire (Napoleon's reign) period in France (1804–20). During the French Revolution, under the influence of the ruling Directory, all ostentatious ornamentation that was associated with the luxury of the court was replaced by straight lines and simplified embellishment. This movement was continued under Napoleon but expanded to include the ornamentation of Egyptian motifs. Empire furniture design was reflected in similar design movements both in England and in America, the latter leading into the American Federal period, characterized by more baroque interpretations of Classic Roman and Greek furniture shapes and ornamentation.

Other lesser design movements followed the Classic era, among them Biedermeier in Germany, a genre featuring heavier lines but simplified ornamentation and utilizing the lighter fruitwoods, and neo-Gothic designs, which were also popular in the middle of the century.

American Empire Chest

Late Nineteenth-Century Victorian

The era that dominated the latter part of the nineteenth century bears the name of the Queen who was so influential in all the fashion trends of her long rule, Victoria. Queen Victoria disdained pretension and formality and the styles that emerged in her period were cozier and more decorative, but often quite rococo, even baroque in interpretation. Walnut, mahogany, rosewood, and walnut were among the favored woods; marble was a popular choice for the tops of tables and cabinets; plush fabrics and decorative tufting were popular looks for upholstery. Actually, Victorian did not represent any pure design concept but was an amalgam of many looks, a hybrid of many design influences.

Victorian Sofa in Louis XV Style

Duncan Phyfe Sewing Table

Twentieth Century

The Art Nouveau movement in furniture design and the Mission style were popular trends in the early part of the twentieth century, this followed by Art Moderne, and ultimately a school that was to have a long and lasting influence on the entire genre of furniture design that is known today as modern or contemporary. This school was the Bauhaus, in Germany, founded in 1919, and the great modern designers who gave this school its great influence were important not only for their innovative styles but also for the ways in which they utilized new methods of manufacture to develop new furniture forms. Among the most famous to come out of the Bauhaus school were Walter Gropius, Marcel Breuer, and Mies Van Der Rohe. The most exciting and prolific period of American furniture design in this century—in the early 1950s during the postwar building boom—owes much of its inspiration to the great classics of this Bauhaus period, many of which are today housed in permanent museum collections.

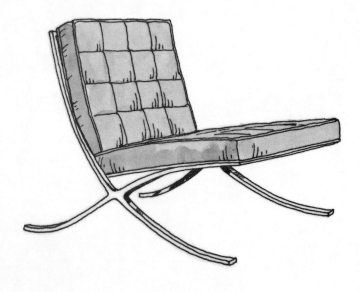

Barcelona Chair

Bertoia Chair

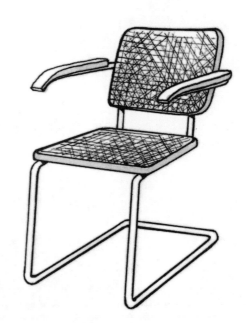

Breuer Chair

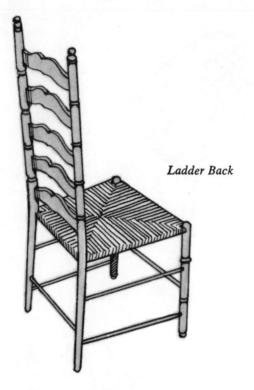

Ladder Back

Bentwood Rocker

Today's contemporary furniture designers continue to draw not only upon examples of the Bauhaus school of design, the classics of the mid-twentieth century, but also continue to reinterpret, modify, and adapt many of the shapes and styles of the seventeenth, eighteenth, and nineteenth centuries.

Country furniture, or country design, is not a style period limited to one specific era of furniture design. Rather it represents a large and comprehensive collection of styles running the gamut of period design influences but rustic and bucolic in inspiration. Country French furniture, for example, comes through as the provincial, simplified, and much cruder interpretations of shapes popular during the reign of Louis XV, while country American includes everything from early pine cupboards fashioned by Colonial carpenters to later Shaker designs, to contemporary pieces fashioned from plainer wood, wicker, rush, and rattan.

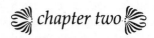

chapter two

Analyze Your Life-Style

To know what you like is a beginning, a good start. But to translate your style preferences into a beautiful, harmonious, comfortable, and *suitable* abode for yourself and your family is the really crucial challenge of interior design. It has to be realistic, practical, and meaningful; it must really work on a round-the-clock basis.

Once you have developed a fairly clear picture of what you like, then talk to the various members of your family and find out what kind of home they would want. Talk about your ideas and basic decorating preferences, and see what kind of reaction you get to these projected suggestions. If you are decorating an entire home or apartment from scratch, then make a list of all your family's needs and requirements, and of every role or roles you want each room to play.

Analyzing your own life-style, if you live alone, or that of your family, if you have one, is not a difficult chore. Simply outline your major living and entertaining habits. Do you prefer formal sit-down dinners or large, casual buffet suppers? Do you have young children, and therefore require sturdy furniture with "childproof" upholstery fabrics? Do you and your husband both work, and therefore need interiors that are easy to keep tidy and clean? Is part of your home to be set up as an at-home office? Does an important hobby suggest that some special area be set aside for its enjoyment?

Where Do You Live?

Where you live and what kind of house you own are also important factors to consider when planning your interiors. A city apartment gets more dirt, grit, and soot than a country or suburban house; it also tends to have less closet and storage space. So it may be very necessary for you to include ample storage furniture as part of your overall plan. If your house or apartment has poor or little natural light, this will influence your choice of colors and patterns, and you will need these elements to lighten and brighten your rooms. On the other hand, if you are decorating a vacation or weekend house, you will want to gear the decorating to the seasonal use of the house. A ski house, for example, would need plenty of extra sleeping facilities, and would be most attractive and inviting if furnished with warm textures and thick carpets. But a leisure home near the beach would require light and bright summery colors, and materials that would withstand the brunt of sun, salt, and sand.

Noise may be a factor if you live in the heart of the city; you may want the aid of wall-to-wall carpeting as insulation, and the muffling qualities of heavy materials chosen for walls or windows. And if you live in a house, remember that your entrance foyer serves not only as the opening statement of your home, it is also a place where snow-covered boots first meet the inside of your house. A practical, easy-care flooring will therefore be a consideration in this instance.

Starting from Scratch or a Simple Re-do

Obviously, a decorating project that starts from scratch is far more time-consuming and all-pervasive than a simple re-do—wherein the furnishings you already own are given a fresh look via possibly a new color scheme, all new upholstery fabrics, change of wall color, etc. While redecoration may involve the planning of a new furniture arrangement, if that is also desired, it does not require the extensive amount of selection and purchasing that must be done to fill completely empty rooms. If you are redecorating because your fabrics are in need of replacement and because you also want a much more attractive and usable home, you should ask yourself and your family the same kind of questions you would throw at them if starting from scratch. But here, you would all try to discover what you do like about your present scheme, what you would like to see changed, what kind of new mood is desirable, what new pieces, if any, should be bought. Show your family photographs of color schemes you feel might work in your present home to get their input. And move around your furniture in your rooms to see if a different arrangement might be more effective and more comfortable.

The Challenge of Moving

In addition to starting from scratch, or redecorating a home in which you now live, are two other possible and challenging decorating situations. One is moving from a small apartment, with a nucleus of furniture, into a larger apartment or spacious home. The second is moving into an apartment from a house with many completely furnished rooms. For the first situation, you would be spreading out, creating entirely new interiors, but at the same time incorporating what you already possess into those new and fresh rooms. The trick here is to accomplish this so well that your home looks as if it had been planned that way, from scratch. In our chapter on furniture arrangement we will deal more fully with this sometimes overwhelming problem. Suffice it to say here that you must again thoroughly analyze your family's lifestyle requirements and the role to which you would assign each room of the new house. The answers that you list will immediately provide you with clues to work out the jigsaw puzzle of combining old furnishings with new purchases. By clarifying your needs, you will also be clarifying your basic approach.

Pare Down if Your New Home Is Smaller

Many people discover, upon moving from a small apartment to a larger house, that some of their furnishings just won't "work" anywhere, in any of the new rooms. So when decorating a first home from scratch, it's an excellent idea to evaluate the flexibility of each item selected. Instead of purchasing sofas, for example, it might make more sense to buy modular seating units that can be rearranged to fit a new floor plan. And why go to the needless expense of installing wall-to-wall carpeting when room-size rugs would be a much more practical and flexible choice? You might even furnish that first apartment with a projected move as an important guideline for many purchases. By assigning future roles to the pieces you buy now, you will eventually be able to purchase what you really want for that new house without making do with undersized furniture or having to replace possessions at a substantial loss.

Retrenching—moving from large quarters to limited ones—can be a more difficult job, especially since it means paring down and eliminating, which can be an arduous emotional, as well as aesthetic and intellectual, process. At some time or other, most of us have visited an older relation, newly moved to a small apartment—and found that aunt or parent literally "buried" under a mountain of furniture that succeeds in making her small abode look like a crowded storage gallery. In order to avoid such a catastrophe, one must be a brutal realist and throw feelings of nostalgia and sentimentality to the winds. Keep all the old photographs you want, but eliminate furniture scientifically and skillfully, using only those pieces that will really work in your new and much smaller home. The best way to do this is to create a floor plan, a furniture arrangement for your new home that makes sense, not only for the fewer and usually smaller rooms, but for your new life-style, which will unquestionably be different from your former one. Then you will immediately see which pieces can be retained and which eliminated. Look upon it as a fresh start, a new beginning.

Storage will probably be one of the most important considerations when you retrench, so make sure that you provide for this when you draw up your new plan. It might even be necessary for you to buy some new furniture, such as modular wall units—which take up space vertically rather than horizontally—when you move to a small apartment. This will not be an exercise in extravagance, but rather a realistic approach to the exigencies of limited space. By selling all the cabinets and dressers you no longer can use, you will have enough to finance such purchases.

Certain things will become obvious to you at once: the big dining-room table can never fit into the small alcove, so a new table—possibly an extension or drop-leaf design—must be purchased. Less obvious are new uses for old pieces that at first thought you might have put on the "sell" list. A tall highboy that cannot fit in the new bedroom might be just the piece to give height and character to a boxy living room, and provide additional storage at the same time. A small writing desk from your former library might be put into service as a nightstand in the new bedroom. So be flexible, do not think of the furniture you already own as being strictly bedroom, living-room, or even dining-room pieces. You may find a new and more interesting use for them in your small apartment.

Whatever kind of decorating project you are managing, always assess the limitations of your rooms, their architectural and spatial flaws or strong points. More of this will be discussed in our section on furniture arrangement.

Avoid Trendy Looks

A final word or two on basic approach. Try to avoid fads and trends, no matter how appealing they may seem to you. Furnish your home with a mood that has "staying power," that will be just as pleasing and meaningful in a year or two as it was when newly installed. Decorate your home for yourself and your family so that it serves as a warm and comfortable nest, not as a status symbol with which to impress friends and relations.

Once you know the basics, you will be able to avoid making any disastrous mistakes, but at the same time keep in mind that there is often more than one possible way to decorate a home to fill your special needs. Be flexible and go slowly, feel free to change and modify as you complete your plan. Decorating is a learning experience, not only when you prepare for it, but as you do it.

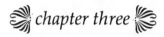

chapter three

Allocate the Budget

There are very few amateur or professional designers for whom price is no object. Each and every one of us has to work within the confines of a limited budget. The point is to make the most out of every decorating dollar, to get your money's worth in terms of wear and tear as well as aesthetic appeal, and to properly allocate the expenditure of the money at your disposal.

Perhaps you have a friend who has been living with an almost bare living room because all the money was put into expensive carpeting and silken wall coverings. Or know someone who spread themselves thin with a lot of low-cost, impractical, and short-lived furnishings, simply because they wanted their home to be decorated "down to the last ashtray." It's hardly necessary to point out here that each extreme is pretty foolish, although at least the person with the empty, carpeted room will eventually own pieces of value.

The Best Approach

Try to establish the amount of money to be spent on the entire house, then break it down, room by room. If you find that one room will cost more than expected, see if you can find some more money from what you budgeted to another area. Often it pays to call in a professional designer to work out a floor plan and budget program for

*Casual and contemporary living room is surprisingly low cost. **What
made this possible were the talents of a skillful do-it-yourselfer, who**
constructed the handsome banquettes from pine planks purchased at a
local lumber yard. Tree trunks are transformed into a glass-topped
table and a pedestal for the seagull sculpture. Wall covering is also of
the hang-it-yourself variety. On the floor is sisal matting, **which is sold**
by the square. Designer is: Dorothy Wyeth Dobbins.*

you. The fee you pay him or her may be well worth the investment, because the designer will immediately be able to give you a realistic price range for every item you hope to buy and also be able to make suggestions for substitutions that may help stretch your dollar. If you are making the bulk of your purchases at a department or furniture store, they will have trained designers on staff who will not only supply you with excellent decorating advice but who can help you develop a practical and effective budget program.

Once you have worked out a sensible budget, you will undoubtedly experience feelings of frustration, a sense of disappointment at not being able to buy immediately what you feel you need. In this case, it might be wise to go over the entire budget and see what pieces you could temporarily eliminate without destroying the charm and usefulness of your home. You might even consider borrowing a piece or two from a member of your family until you can afford the design of your dreams. If you're a newlywed, don't be ashamed of including some carry-over pieces from your own apartment (or that of your spouse's) because it doesn't live up to your ideal plan. Since you expect eventually to replace these pieces, use them for the moment to stretch your budget, so that you can better afford to invest in the other pieces that you desperately need.

How to Stretch the Budget

Being resourceful in other ways can also help your budget problems. Plan to buy furniture, linens, accessories, and carpeting at those seasons when most stores feature special sales. Unless you feel the need to buy everything "brand new," you might be able to find some great "steals" at local garage sales and auctions of quality secondhand furniture. And don't be afraid of accepting a wonderful gift just because it doesn't quite fit into your original decorating concept. If your mother offers you a marvelous oriental rug, when you had planned on wall-to-wall carpeting, try to rearrange your decorating plan—perhaps by using more plain textures rather than patterned prints—to accommodate a different kind of floor treatment. You might end up liking it more than the first approach.

It's very possible that either you or your spouse is a talented home handyman, without even knowing it. Buying secondhand furniture, and then stripping and refinishing it, is one great way of stretching the

A wonderful alternative to the usual large painting over the sofa, and much more unusual but less costly, is this blowup of a photograph, divided into thirds and then separately framed and hung low over modular seat units. Any professional color lab can make such a modern "triptych" from one of your own negatives. A landscape, such as this, is an excellent subject for such a treatment.

budget and also of creating furnishings that are very personal, one-of-a-kind designs. Built-in storage is not as complicated as it may seem, especially if one of you has some training in carpentry. New strippable, self-gluing wall coverings come in a whole world of fabulous patterns and textures. By putting up such a paper yourselves, instead of calling in a professional to install a more costly quality, you will have saved a great deal of money and yet achieved an equally charming effect. Another reason not to buy expensive wall covering is short-term use. If you are planning a move in the near future, paint your walls and put your money into furnishings that can move with you.

But be realistic about any attempts at doing-it-yourself. Time is worth money, and if you can't really handle a simple project, it will probably make more sense to call in a professional, or simplify your original scheme and do without it altogether.

A word of caution about budget stretching. What you should aim for in furnishing your home is good value—furnishings that will last, that will serve their time. Don't scrimp or try to cut corners when purchasing major items—bedding, sofas, upholstered furniture, cabinets, dressers, etc. What you should be searching for is value—long-lasting value, rather than a super-low price tag. If you are lucky enough to come across a quality item that has been marked way down because it has been discontinued or is a showroom sample that has been upholstered in a fabric that you love and can use but that others might find limiting (hence the discount), buy this piece by all means. But check construction, guarantees, materials used, and manufacturers' labels when purchasing those items from which you want value received. Buying from a reputable store or furniture gallery is another way of ensuring good value, because you know you can return something easily if anything goes wrong.

There are ways of getting around a budget without completely sacrificing your mood. If you can't afford both a country French armoire and a four-poster bed, buy just the armoire—it will be important enough in size to convey the mood you want to establish. Buy only bedding on a movable frame for now, improvising possibly with a canopy effect that is a simple wall construction. Or use a skirted table in the living room in place of that expensive end table you hoped to buy. Have the skirt made of a fabric that matches a pattern or print used on upholstered furniture or for draperies. This kind of substitute will not destroy your overall effect.

Buy Less Now, Add More Later

Instead of buying all those seating modules or storage units you felt you needed, buy a few less if the design is offered on an open-stock basis. You can add later, and in the meantime the additional money can be put into something else even more necessary at the moment. If your apartment is only a temporary living place—for two or three years—then avoid investing in elaborate wall covering or carpeting, background investments or on any improvements that you can't take with you.

You may have to rethink your entire plan if it turns out that you will end up with a very bare-looking home, even if you try to stretch your dollars as wisely as you can. A bold color scheme, the generous use of a strong pattern or print can go a long way toward filling up space visually if not actually. So you might consider changing that understated and monochromatic scheme into something a little more lively in order to make your home seem more fully furnished than it actually is. Filling in with inexpensive wall decor, such as large posters that you can frame yourself, is still another way of cutting down on a bare and empty look.

It is important that your first home or apartment be part of an overall plan, that its furnishings serve you well at this present way station and also function usefully in future homes. Don't feel defensive or apologetic if your home isn't quite the dream place you imagined it to be. Because it really shouldn't be a perfect answer, unless the sky's the limit. If you chose everything just to suit that first apartment, you might end up with a certain amount of inflexibility—furnishings that really won't work well in the next home.

Your present decor should suit your station in life, your age, your life-style. If you have to improvise a bit, so be it. Many middle-aged couples look back with pleasure at those days when they survived with orange crates or had all their friends over for a paint-the-house party!

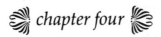

chapter four

Pick a Starting Point

Once you have analyzed your life-style and have assessed the role that each room in your home must play, you should have a good idea of the kind of mood, the implicit character that each will have. Part of this, of course, is determined by the kind of furniture you expect to buy —warm, country pieces, sleek streamlined designs, gracious traditional classics, and so on. But the way you use this furniture, the personal expression of taste that will come through in choice of color scheme, room arrangement, accessories, wall decoration, and so on will intensify or modify the mood already established by the style of furniture. If your basic furniture designs are modern, will you go all out with a sleek modern theme or soften it with many antique and traditional accent pieces? Do you prefer to use contemporary textures with your Early American designs or do you want a purer kind of American look?

You May "Own" a Starting Point

One of the best ways to key the character of your room and also get you moving with the entire decorating plan is to find a starting point, one design element that will immediately establish the direction in which you expect to go. This starting point may be something you already own or something you intend to buy. The possibilities are endless. It could be a family heirloom—a hand-painted cabinet, a grandfather clock, an Aubusson rug, a Coramandel screen. Or something you have collected or splurged on before you got married—an abstract painting, blue and white Canton ware serving pieces, a Victorian file cabinet. If you have designed and crafted a bevy of needlepoint pillows over the years, these too could function as a helpful starting point. So could a personal collection of Czechoslovakian art glass, or country baskets, or Japanese Imari ware.

If you don't possess these kinds of starting points, you may already own them in your mind. If, for example, you will settle for nothing less than a deeply tufted Chesterfield sofa, then buy one and build your room around it. If you long for one of those ravishingly colored neo-traditional floral prints, hunt one down, and let this be the focal point of your color scheme. If you've always preferred oriental rugs to plain carpets, make a rug the first thing you buy, then take the style and color cue from its pattern.

Wallpaper, fabric prints, and patterns, even paintings, are ready-made ways to begin a color scheme. You might find a pattern that while you don't intend to use it in your home presents to you exactly the combination of colors you wish to use.

A starting point can also be a top priority in your list of purchases. If your family are bookworms, then you'll need plenty of bookshelves; this will determine how much additional cabinetry for which there will be space. If a den or family room is to serve also as a television room and study for the man of the house, look for a wonderful tweed or plaid and build from there. For a family who entertains often and spontaneously, plenty of comfortable upholstered furniture should be the starting point for the major living areas.

Use Essentials As Your Building Blocks

Try to avoid one common trap of starting a new decorating venture. Do not feel that you have to begin with a specific possession just because you have invested a great deal of money in it. It may have worked beautifully in your last home, but be too big, too small, or just the wrong shape, size, pattern, or look for your present apartment. Don't build on it; eliminate it. Favorite possessions are an almost foolproof way of giving a home personal character and warmth, but if they are inadequate to your present needs, then start afresh. Otherwise

REPRINTED FROM BRIDE's. COPYRIGHT © 1978 BY THE
CONDÉ NAST PUBLICATIONS INC.

op) Radiant blue and white living space
 designer Gary Crain incorporates
ning and sleeping areas within the con-
es of one large room. Sleeping alcove is
 on a raised platform; oval dining
le fits neatly into one corner. Blues
ige from rich sapphire tones to the paler
es of dhurrie rug and throw pillows.
vo superbold accents—the red shawl and
 "Joseph's Coat" bed quilt—are
lcome intrusions.

(Bottom) An abstract painting of jumbo
proportions livens a low-key living room
that teams warm putty tones with deep
blacks. Designer Bebe Winkler, who
created the sculpture-shaped coffee table,
planned this room for casual comfort
and ease of care. Accessories such as
throw pillows and shawl add softening
touches.

(Top) The lively patterns or zingy colors that are available in today's bed linens make possible the new "undressed" bed, a much easier way to live—with no heavy bedcovers to take off or put on. This sparkling modern bedroom designed by Gary Crain features angled placement of platform bed for a more interesting utilization of space.

(Bottom) Geometric wallpaper stripe covers walls and ceilings of a modest-size bedroom that appears more spacious than it really is. This is due to compact and streamlined built-in storage and study areas and trim, platform-supported bed. Roman blinds provide sleek and space-saving window dressing. Interior by Robert Metzger.

PHOTOGRAPHED BY FELICIANO.
BELL SYSTEMS TRIMLINE TELEPHONE

FIXTURES AND ACCESSORIES BY SHERLE WAGNER INTERNATIONAL, INC.

FASHON® WALLCOVERINGS BY GENERAL TIRE/GTR WALLCOVERING CO.

op) One provocative attern, a dhurrie rug nployed as a bedcover, jects soft blues and arm terra cottas into a om that is otherwise hite. Bebe Winkler, who signed this interior and e funiture in it, loves to le pillows at the head of bed for a look of luxe d super comfort.

(Left) The ultimate in sybaritic luxury is possible even when a bathroom is quite small. Here crystal sconces, framed mirrors, porcelain-trimmed fixtures, hand-painted washbasin, and marble counter top create an interior of unsurpassed elegance and color excitement. Design by Zauderer-Duchin Associates.

(Right) Antique shaving stand, lace-trimmed towels, and dressmaker touches evoke a nostalgic and appealing Victorian charm in a bathroom that demonstrates the power of simple "facelifting" when a complete remodeling job is beyond the budget. Pretty floral wall covering, which covers the ceiling too, adds to the sense of space.

(Top Left) Dazzling coats of butter-yellow paint and matching linens do wonders to an older bathroom with vintage fixtures. Even the outmoded bathtub becomes a "collector's piece" instead of an eyesore. Whimsical and washable wall coverings that feature sketches of yesterday's baths integrate the chopped-up wall areas of this tiny room.

(Bottom) Studies show that small babies love and respond to brilliant zingy colors. So designer Edmund Motyka concentrated on vibrant hues of blue, yellow, and red for a dazzling interior that should please any tot's appetite for scintillating hues. Built-in bookshelves form a niche for the crib, decorated with a mural made from paper cutouts.

(Top Right) Lively linen capitalize on two of the boldest colors in the scrubbable, scrapbook-inspired wall-covering design whose pattern is strong enough to provide a vintage bathroom with a fresh personality. Since wall space is so limited, the standing towel rack is a welcome addition.

you may find that you have created an entire room that doesn't work because it's been built around a possession no longer right for you.

The starting points we have dealt with thus far have been primarily style and color cues, devices upon which to build the style and mood of your home. There are also the basic elements you will need, many of which you can also use as the primary building blocks of each room plan. While we will deal at length with the kind and style of furniture chosen for each room in those chapters devoted to furniture selection and arrangement, and specific room requirements, mention should also be made about the order in which one goes about furnishing a room.

If you and your husband require a king-size bed, for example, then the entire plan of your bedroom must start with that. The need for some kind of desk or study area can start you off on your floor plan for the living room. If you often have overnight guests (parents from out of town) in your small apartment, then you might consider buying a sofa bed for the dining alcove and creating another place to dine within the living room proper. Hence, a sleep sofa and a drop-leaf table might serve as starting points for your apartment. If you and your husband are television addicts, obviously some place must be established for a television set; this decision will determine how the rest of the room will lay out. A large wardrobe will require ample storage space; you might want to find the appropriate storage cabinet or cabinets before you proceed with other selections.

Limitations Can Give a Focus

Precise needs, such as the ones outlined above, are more limiting when an apartment or home is small and has few rooms. It will not be as crucial to use them as pivotal choices if you live in a spacious home with lots of rooms, but it is still advisable to keep these priorities in mind, even when space is no problem. Zeroing in first on the essentials, on what you need or feel you must have, is always an excellent way to begin any design project, no matter how big or how small.

Surprisingly, you will discover that certain limitations or stipulated requirements can give direction and focus to your decorating plan. Sometimes it's much more difficult to settle on a basic approach when you can do almost anything you want. Special needs, personal living and style requirements can ease the way, can give immediate shape and meaning to your entire decorating project.

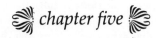

chapter five

Develop a Color Sense

Color has magic, a magic that nourishes the eye and delights the senses. To view a riot of colors in a June flower garden or in the brush strokes of a painting is surely a tonic for the soul. And we can take this magic, manipulating it wisely and well, to endow our interiors with the substance and sparkle that make them warm, radiant, memorable, and enduringly comfortable. For color is a tool, the most plentiful and least expensive decorating tool around. Once, costly dyeing techniques limited the choice and availability of color; today, modern technology and the development of synthetics that express color with the sharpest clarity provide color selection in almost overwhelming profusion. The home-furnishings world is a veritable bazaar of colors and color combinations of such variety and scope that we can be easily confused and overpowered. From this great richness of choice, what do we choose for our own homes, where do we begin?

Exploit Color Power

The power of color to shape a room is what makes it so effective; it is also what fills many people with trepidation, for fear that they may use color in the wrong way. So rather than exploiting color potential to its fullest, they play it safe. This often results in rooms that are dull and prosaic, in spite of beautiful furnishings and cohesive decorating.

Color can titillate, it can soothe, it can unify or divide, it can create visual interest or serve as camouflage. It can give scope and scale to a small room or make a spacious one seem warmer and more intimate. It can hide architectural flaws and defects, dramatize beautiful embellishments. It can integrate a room of disparate furniture styles; it can express a very personal point of view.

How to choose colors, how to combine them, and then how to implement them to produce the desired effect can be skillfully approached only after one has first understood what color is, what the basic relationships between one color family and another are, and what the key characteristics of each color tend to be.

A knowledge of what color is can be gleaned from a basic study of the color wheel. These basic ABCs can hone your skill in selecting colors, in combining colors, and in allocating them, in using color for accent, as a device to cool or warm, to enlarge space or diminish it.

The Basic Color Wheel

The primary colors are red, yellow, blue. These are pure colors; they do not derive from a mixture of colors. They are the three basics.

The secondary colors are green (yellow and blue), orange (red and yellow), purple (blue and red). These three secondary colors are produced by the mixture of two primary colors.

The tertiary colors are blue-green, yellow-green, yellow-orange, red-orange, red-purple, blue-purple. These six tertiary colors result from the mix of a primary color with an adjacent secondary color.

There are basically, then, twelve colors in the palette, but there are many, many other colors in the decorator's portfolio. Color tints—the degree of white added—and color variations—the amount and choice of secondary color or colors that are used for the mixes—have created an almost unlimited range of color possibilities.

The Big Six

Each of the three primary and the three secondary colors, pure, and in their infinite variations, have specific characteristics that provide a special chemistry for the alchemy of color decoration.

Yellow

Buttercups dancing in a windswept field, lemons bunched in a straw basket, a child's painting of the morning sun, a golden bangle bracelet —all are forms of yellow, bouncing and boisterous in its sharper and spicier variations, rich, luminous, burnished in its more mellow shades. Yellow can turn a dark and dreary room into a setting of piquant sparkle or give dimension and strength to an interior filled with the palest naturals.

Add red or orange to yellow and you strengthen its impact; use white to clarify or sharpen yellow, or use black as a fascinating counterpoint.

Orange

The afterglow of a setting sun, the lushness of ripe peaches, a slice of glistening cantaloupe, the shocking mane of carrot-colored hair, tawny tones of pumpkin and squash—all shades of scintillating orange, a color that exhilarates, uplifts, adds an inimitable flavor, even as a minor accent. Neutrals can soften orange; adjacent primaries of red and yellow turn its power acid-sharp. Green endows orange with garden-fresh shimmer, blue tames and leavens it, adding propensities for sophistication and elegance. Orange can wake up a room of browns, explode the chemistry of black with white.

Red

A speeding fire engine, a flock of cardinals zooming south, a weathered barn, or clay pots on a windowsill—all attest to the unchallenged reign of red, the supreme, effortless, and quintessentially boldest hue in the color spectrum. A tiny bit goes a long way, although a room of reds can be surprisingly elegant and sumptuous. Red's variations are indeed infinite, stretching from the deepest crimsons and carnelians to the iciest, coolest of pinks.

Red is not for the timid, but it is certainly a healing tonic for timid, nondescript rooms. Partnered with yellow, red can be boisterous; with beiges and browns, red shows character; and with gold and white, it displays its regal manners. Red can invest traditional furnishings with contemporary pizzazz or give needed emotional comfort to a hard-edged modern room.

Purple

Like red, its closest neighbor on the color wheel, purple has the vigor to dominate when used full strength. Diluted and softened with other colors, it undergoes disarming transformations, changing into aubergine, lilac, hyacinth, magenta, and plum. Add blue and purple cools down; with red it assumes a royal or romantic pose. Purple can be the catalyst that prevents a room of neutrals from being dull; it can join an equal strength of green for a crisp and urbane look. Purple can create exotic effects when balanced with pinks and yellows or can be subtle when tempered with browns and golds.

Blue

An abiding favorite, an easy companion to many colors, blue is also the color of sky and sea, of sapphires and lapis lazuli, of irises and delphiniums, of opalines and turquoises. White magnifies blue, red pulls it closer to purple. And blue and white become the most popular partnership of the day, because the combination both soothes and refreshes. Add colors to this steady duo: yellow, and the look is sunnier; green and the theme is garden fresh; red, for a patriotic medley; or peach for a new kind of elegance.

Green

The feathers of a parrot, the lacquerlike shell of an avocado, lettuce, limes, a mossy patch in the forest, malachite, a mint julep, a velvet lawn—green is all these things, sometimes lively and animated, often serene and subdued, but always a handsome and richly satisfying color. Frequently chosen, because of its versatility and limitless variations, green also changes tune with each partner. With yellow, melon, or apricot, it becomes warmer, more sparkling, a glowing radiance. With blue, in an analogous pairing, it can be sleek and chic. Green brings the lushness of nature into any room, whether expressed in wall covering or upholstery fabrics or in a proliferation of potted plants. Green was as popular hundreds of years ago as it is today, reminding us within our homes of the brightest and freshest hues of the world outside. Greens go well together, and green laced with white can be the crispest, springiest look of all.

White and the Neutrals

Even a poster-bright room depends upon white and/or neutrals for areas of counterpoint or quiet. It is how we use color in concert with these "no-color" hues that will determine the total color impact in any room.

White

White is familiar to most as a companion or auxiliary "color," not as a color in its own right. But it can be just that: witness the all-white rooms that have become a hallmark of contemporary decorating in the last forty years. And while white was once an unthinkable choice for the practical-minded, today white is offered with easy-care potential due to new soil-resistant finishes and features and washable synthetic textures. The white silk curtains of yesterday were never as white as the machine-washable polyesters of today, so now we have even whiter whites with which to work. White is also a chameleon; it changes with each texture. The white of fur is unlike the white of marble; a lacquered table has a different whiteness from a cotton weave from Haiti or a shiny ceramic-tile floor. White can clarify and dramatize, can open up space, present a masterful sense of luxe, let paintings or posters dominate a room. And, of course, white works beautifully with every color in the rainbow, as well as with itself. White, pared with black, is a recurring theme in traditional and modern rooms, a provocative combination when used alone or as a backdrop to jewel-bright accents.

The Neutrals

There are very few color schemes that do not include at least one neutral—that whole, easygoing family of low-key hues ranging from the palest ecru through silver, sandalwood, nutria, and charcoal—every shade that derives from a mix of brown with white or black with white. The beginner will discover that the formula of neutrals-plus-a-color is one of the easiest to develop and apply. It is not only a "safe" approach but a flexible one as well. Neutrals such as beige, straw, cinnamon, and oyster white can be used for large areas such as wall color, carpeting, drapery fabric and sofa texture, while a colorful accent, such as bristol blue or parrot green, can be chosen for pillows, a pull-up chair, a few accessories, and so on. To change the mood of this scheme would simply require a change of accessories, new pillows, and some minor reupholstery. Neutrals-plus-a-color schemes have great staying power; they are not the kinds of combinations of which one tires easily. The degree to which one introduces the strong color will determine just how low-key or how lively the arrangement will be. Neutral schemes are often preferable for rooms filled with beautifully crafted furniture —possibly antiques and a collection of valuable paintings—so that the graining of beautiful woods and the colors of cherished canvases can be properly enjoyed.

Color Schemes

Color schemes break down, basically, into the following categories: TRIADIC (three colors equidistant from each other on the wheel); COMPLEMENTARY (colors at opposite ends of the wheel); ANALOGOUS (related colors, those next to each other on the wheel); MONOCHRO-MATIC (one color in a range of values and intensities); and MULTI-COLOR (schemes using more than three colors).

Now that you're better acquainted with the color wheel, and with the special characteristics or properties of each color family, it's time to use this information to develop the color schemes for the room or rooms of your home.

Create Your Scheme

How do you go about it? First, by using the same self-discovery methods you applied when searching out your design and style prefer-ences. Go through books and magazines, visit model rooms and deco-rator showcase houses. Cut out and collect photographs of color schemes that please and warm you. Next, go out in the market—to de-partment and fabric stores, wallpaper shops, paint suppliers. Get swatches of fabric or paper prints with color schemes that really "grab" you, bring home paint chips and samples of rug colors. When you get all this together, don't be surprised to see that you've repeated yourself and, like a homing pigeon, have returned again and again to certain kinds of color themes. This will tell you a lot about your color fancies. But don't stop there. Put all your photos, swatches, and samples into a scrapbook or folder and show them to your family, eliminating immediately any that they dislike. If one of the rooms is being designed for a specific member of the family, such as a son or daughter, make sure that they have a strong voice in the selection of their own color plan, but show them your own suggestions first.

Once you have narrowed down the color preferences, you have begun to shape your color schemes. But this is only a beginning. For many other significant factors come into play that will influence your final choice, that will make you select one scheme and discard another.

In the first place, are you decorating a small apartment or a rambling house? If the first, then aim for a scheme that tends to enlarge space, to create a flow of color from one area to another. A tiny apartment is not the place for a series of different color schemes—nothing will succeed faster at making your home seem pint-sized and cramped. Choose instead either a monochromatic scheme or a two-color plan, possibly with one minor accent hue—and continue this single plan throughout your space. You could introduce a certain amount of variation to keep the total effect from being monotonous or boring. If your color scheme is blue, white, and yellow, you could use white as the most important color in the living room, with blue second and yellow for accent. An adjacent bedroom could be yellow and white, with blue playing only a minor role. An entrance foyer or small dining area could be predominately blue, using yellow and white for accent.

For a larger house, you can indulge in more than one basic scheme, especially if the house has two stories. Upstairs bedrooms do not have to relate to what has happened below, but even in a large house it is a good idea to have some relationship in the color plan of adjacent rooms, so that you do not experience the shock of stepping from one color plan into a totally different one, or viewing through a large doorway colors that clash with the ones near at hand. Color should flow easily and unobtrusively from one room or area to another.

Role of Lighting and Climate

Climate and lighting also play an important role in the selection and formation of a color scheme. You may welcome the warming colors of red and orange for a house in the mountains, while preferring the cooling tones of blue, pale yellow, and leaf green for a beach house or a getaway in the tropics.

Does your color plan have to compensate for poor or limited natural light? A plan of slate grays and somber browns would hardly be the proper choice for a room with little natural light. By the same token, you would want to tone down an interior with a southern exposure and many large windows—one that enjoys the benefit of bright daylight and sunlight most of the time.

A northern exposure tends to make a room seem cold, so select the warmest scheme from your scrapbook to make it cozy and hospitable. Scarlet draperies and carpets were often favored in period bedrooms that lacked the warmth of central heating—to offset, at least visually and psychologically, the physical coldness of these rooms.

It's a good rule of thumb to use moderate color schemes in rooms that enjoy a lot of use. The major living space in a small apartment might be the candidate for a scheme of neutrals, one that is easy on the eye, less tiresome. On the other hand, a large dining room used primarily for elegant dinner parties might be just the place to indulge in a vibrant and fanciful scheme. Bold wallpaper colors, a zingy rug, splashy table linens will establish the mood for festive, gala dining.

Serene Colors for Study, Relaxation

Avoid bold and animated colors in rooms intended for study or rest — a den or home office, a bedroom used only for sleeping. Soft and muted colors add a sense of relaxation and provide a restful backdrop for work or study. The same is true of a kitchen—shocking colors tend to slow down the pace of food preparation and clean-up.

Certain colors convey a mood of formality, others are more casual. Pretty hues, such as pink, pale blue, and other pastels tend to look feminine, while "earth" colors such as olive, brown, and deep apricot can produce a more masculine mood.

Analyze the use time of a specific room. If it's strictly a daytime room, then evaluate your color plan in terms of natural lighting. An evening room, on the other hand, will be viewed mainly in artificial light. Test your colors under the corresponding conditions before you make your final selections.

Allocation of color is not a simple procedure but one that requires a great deal of advance planning. Go through your scrapbook and pick out at least three variations of your basic color scheme. Note that in each there will be a somewhat different allocation of the basic color, the green, let us say, dominating in one, the blue in another. Use color in proportion to the intensity of color desired. If you want a low-key effect, then use your softer, neutral colors on the larger expanses—floors, walls, larger upholstered pieces such as sofas and sectionals. For a bolder effect, use a bright color on at least one major piece, or possibly one wall area. Avoid a spotty effect such as applying a bold color in a hit-and-miss fashion. Remember that bright and dark colors advance, pale and soft hues recede. Utilize this information if you need to make a room seem larger or smaller than it actually is. Receding colors can lift a ceiling or broaden a narrow room; advancing colors lower a ceiling and create a more intimate mood.

Color Dramatizes Architectural Features

Analyze the architecture of a room. Awkward jogs or beams, often found in tract houses or high-rise apartments, and protruding radiators and air-conditioners, a common condition in older layouts, can be "blotted out" with the same sweep of color chosen for wall paint. Handsome and deeply recessed windows, decorative molding on the other hand, often deserve to be outlined with a color that provides a dramatic contrast to the wall tone.

If your room already has its share of browns, in wall paneling and parquet flooring, then you might opt for a color scheme that provides some relief—a pale or vibrant plan rather than one that offers more of the same.

As a collector of modern abstract paintings, colorful handcrafts, or unusual accessories, you would be more likely to prefer a color theme that allows the marvelous hues of canvases or collectibles to come through rather than have them "wiped out" by an overpowering combination of colors.

Magnificent antiques, the rich patina of gorgeously grained woods and veneers do not warrant the competition of attention-getting color schemes. As suggested earlier, a more subtle approach is advised, so that possessions such as these can be properly seen and appreciated. On the other hand, a superbright, instant-impact color scheme can compensate for an underfurnished room or one filled with low-cost, makeshift furniture. The power of color to entertain the eye distracts from the limitations or sparsity of the furnishings.

Pitfalls to Avoid

There are no "wrong" colors in nature or in the color spectrum, but there are wrong, frequently disastrous ways to use and combine color. Try to avoid the most common pitfalls of the color-scheme game. First of all, stay away from faddish, trendy color combinations, just as you would try to avoid gimmicky furniture designs and decorating techniques that are in one season, out the next. Don't get carried away by the fascinating and innovative color ideas of a magazine photo or model room. Very often this is done for entertainment value; such rooms are not to be taken seriously as places in which to live. If used at all, these schemes are better left to the professionals who have the expertise to temper and adapt them.

In planning your scheme, don't limit yourself to the concept that a traditional room merits a period color theme, unless, of course, you want a purist, museum-authentic interpretation. It may be that you would like to give your traditional furniture a fresh and young look. If that's the case, a more contemporary color scheme might be just the answer.

Above all, don't be like the fanatic who goes from store to store with a paint chip in order to find an upholstery or drapery fabric that is an "exact match." Textural differences preclude this kind of scientific exactness, as mentioned before, but aside from this, why spend that kind of sweat and energy hunting down perfect matches? A certain amount of variation creates a much more interesting and personal room; the exact-match look tends to be sterile.

Be sure to collect large swatches of fabrics, wallpapers, prints, etc., for your color portfolio; they will give you a much more accurate reading than tiny scraps. Do not stand too close to a woven or printed pattern in evaluating its suitability; get the overall color impression from a certain amount of distance, as this will be how such a pattern will be seen in the room.

Do not nail down your color scheme until you complete the projected furniture selection and arrangement plan, since you will not be able to "position" the various colors until this has been done. Use your large rug and fabric swatches to place color, play around with them, try them out in different locations. If you seem to have a choice, go with the scheme that seems a little more daring, a little bolder. Color schemes tend to "make up" as less vibrant than they seem in sample form.

Have fun with color; don't fight it but make the most of it. Above all, use those colors and color combinations that work best for you, for your house, for each room, and for each member of your family. If you tire of that purple dress in a few seasons, it's no disaster. But when you invest in costly home furnishings, and wrap all of these in a specific color plan, make sure that plan continues to please the eye and the emotions of the family that lives within it.

part two

THE ABCs OF PLANNING AHEAD

Introduction

At this point, the world of decorating should no longer seem foreign or incomprehensible. You have gotten your feet wet by studying the designs of past and present, analyzing your life-style (and that of your family), developed a realistic approach to how and where the money is to be spent, sorted out your color preferences and priorities, gotten a pretty good idea of what is available and how much it costs. Your scrapbook of photographs, swatches, chips, and samples is full to overflowing, but further planning is still ahead before you can nail down a finished decorating plan. Now you must start to narrow the choices, and as you pare down, you will begin to build a structure, a decorating discipline for each and every room. To do this you should organize all of your material, creating separate folders for each room to be decorated, much the way professional designers approach each one of their jobs. In each folder you will not only file the appropriate style moods and color schemes but also possible suggestions for background decorations, window treatments, fabric selections, floor-covering textures and patterns, furniture designs, type or kind of pieces required, and room arrangements or floor plans. Special prerequisites such as ample storage, dual-purpose furniture, built-in lighting, and free-standing illumination should also be part of each portfolio where they apply. Last but far from least will be clippings of the kinds of accessories you will buy, how they will be placed or showcased (if you plan to include any kind of collection).

Soon we will be taking you through the basics of decorating every kind of room (living room, dining room, bedroom, family room, etc.) in your home. But before we reach this phase of room decoration, we must first become familiar with the enormous number of options available for each aspect of a room's decoration, exploring the decorative potential of each background element, home furnishings product, furniture, and style and type of design—as well as how to arrive at the best possible furniture arrangement or floor plan. When we have absorbed all of this, and sifted out those choices that are most appropriate for our special needs, we will then be able to finalize the decorating-game plan, room by room.

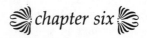

chapter six

Backgrounds— Walls

Backgrounds can make the difference between a merely attractive interior and one with substance and character. Dull, sterile architecture can diminish the warmth, interest, and decorative impact of a room's furnishings, no matter how beautiful or how skillfully put together. Of course, high-cost modern houses with their walls of glass and innovative spatial concepts are quite naturally built without these traditional embellishments; they have a sleek and streamlined style of their own. But the typical box, the lackluster room of a tract house or new apartment, offers neither period ornamentation of older structures nor the marvelous airiness of architect-designed custom homes. To compensate, we must often add background elements of our own to bring the backdrop of the room up to the charm and quality of the furniture and accessories.

Have you ever walked through a department store and observed a model room in an early stage of decoration? Walls have been papered, a fireplace added, windows are draped, the floor carpeted. The room is unfinished, yet it already has a style, a personality. If you can do the same thing with your empty rooms—give them a style before you add a single piece of furniture—then you have succeeded in creating an effective stage or backdrop for your interior.

Assess the Role of Your Walls

A number of years ago, a New York City designer became a legend in her own time by showing darkly painted or paneled, or richly patterned fabric-covered walls, after an extended era of whitewashed anonymous wall treatment. Giving walls greater importance, whether with strong wall color or pattern, with the sparkle of mirrors or the warmth and texture of paneling, can make all the difference in the essential ambiance of a room.

The choices are many, but one does not go ahead and use background materials willy-nilly because they "are there." Background embellishment adds considerably to the cost of a job, even if you do the installation yourself. The walls of the rooms should be assessed and evaluated before any background changes are made. What role are they to play in the scheme of things—provide the rich patina of wood in a family room or serve as a subtle background for beautiful paintings in a living room? Are the walls badly cracked and marred, and therefore in dire need of a renewing cover? Can the poor proportions of a setting benefit from the skillful use of paint, the attention-getting propensities of a lively wallpaper pattern? Does the period style of the furniture require the enrichment of decorative moldings? Is the wall treatment to be used to visually magnify the space of a room or make it seem smaller and cozier?

Paint is, of course, the first decorating tool that comes to mind in the decoration of walls—it's inexpensive, can be easily and quickly applied, and is a foolproof way of giving a room a fresh and clean look.

Most people play it safe with paint color, as well they should if a subtle backdrop is specifically required. But paint can also be a powerful and flexible decorating tool that can be manipulated to create certain effects, solve special problems, alter a room's personality.

We have already touched upon much of this in our chapter dealing with the special decorating properties of color. Wall paint can thereby be exploited to make color do its work—push walls back or bring them forward, lower ceilings or raise them, give decorative impact to a room filled with makeshift furniture. And more specifically, paint can be employed to dramatize beautiful molding, emphasize a fireplace wall, divide space in a room, or blot out eyesores such as radiators or odd jogs and beams or even create spectacular wall graphics.

The ceiling is usually white or continues the color of the walls, unless a specific effect is desired, as mentioned above. A word to the wise should be made here. Don't exploit the space-changing power of paint color unless it works best for the overall plan. Perhaps you like a small room's intimacy and do not want or need to use a pale paint color to extend the walls. Why drop a ceiling with a dark coat of paint unless that, too, blends in with the desired effect? No paint color in the world is going to transform undersized boxes into huge interiors, so apply the space-modifying properties of paint color only where really desired.

And don't be guided by the chip alone. A large wall will "read" very differently from a tiny paint sample. Invest in a pint of the paint color you think is right, then apply it to a few square feet of wall space. This should give you a much better idea of how the paint color operates on the walls and in your room. Always remember that dried paint is usually a lighter shade than the same paint in the can.

Divide with Color

We said something earlier about using paint to divide an area. This is especially useful when an apartment has no entry; one just steps into the living room. To create a sense of foyer, a totally different color wall paint can "recess" the walls near the front door. Naturally the color should relate to a tone planned for the area's color scheme. A change in wall color can help to separate a dining ell or alcove from the adjacent living area. But it will also chop up the space visually. With a mixed blessing, such as this approach, weigh the advantages and disadvantages as they apply to your needs before deciding.

Special effects, such as striped woodwork or bold wall graphics, are best left to the professional designers who can give painters the guidance they need and who will be in a better position to assess whether or not treatments such as these are warranted. Avoid the gimmicky—one wall of bold color—and dark trendy hues such as sepia or eggplant for large expanses and well-lived-in rooms unless you really know what you are doing. The only thing that can be said for paint mistakes—they can be erased with a new color, but then you've thrown out the money paid for the first try.

Wall Coverings—Paper and Fabric

The basic difference in walls covered with paper or fabric is one of texture. Even a smooth fabric has subtle texture and depth. Paper, except for flocked designs or those laminated with some kind of material such as straw, silk, or grasscloth, does not.

Wallpaper is one of the marvelous ways of endowing a room with instant drama and pattern interest, a wonderful tonic for a room of bland and sterile architecture. But because strongly patterned walls tend to dominate, restrict them to rooms of limited use, such as kitchens, foyers, and guest bathrooms, or areas where you desire a dramatic effect, such as dining rooms. Of course wallpapers come in small-scale, subtly colored interpretations, and these can be used in almost any area of the home, even in small rooms. A tiny bedroom sheathed in the same wallpaper print on walls and ceiling—with matching fabric used for the window treatment—can be a charming jewel.

Wallpaper is especially effective in covering stained or cracked walls; they do not require as much plastering or preparation, although most paperhangers will use a lining to cover blemished walls before they paper.

Once you explore the wall-covering market, you will more than likely be overwhelmed by an embarrassment of riches. The choice of pattern, color, scale, and style is veritably endless. Not only that, but today many wall coverings are made of vinyl or are vinyl-faced so that they are easy to scrub clean. Many papers are "strippable" and can be removed and reused in a new abode, and even more are offered with a self-adhesive and need only to be wetted down before being applied. If you would like to save the cost of a paperhanger and do it yourself, try out your expertise on a closet to find out whether or not you can handle the job.

Wallpaper Patterns

Obviously you must choose a wallpaper in conjunction with other pattern selections. A dominant wallpaper motif will limit you to plain textures in drapery and upholstery fabrics unless you plan to use matching or correlating prints. Be careful here not to overdo a good thing, or to select a wallpaper design that really doesn't work with the style of your furniture or mood of your room, even if it is especially appealing to you.

The principle of small-scale wallpaper for small rooms and large-scale for large areas is fine insofar as it goes, but don't be afraid to "break the rules" when a change of pace is indicated. A bold mural or a generously proportioned *trompe l'oeil* design might be just the answer for a small entrance hall that can use a dramatic accent and strong decorative interest, especially when there is little room for any furniture. Remember, also, that wallpaper patterns seem bolder in a wallpaper showroom or store than they do on the wall. If you have to choose between a pattern or color that seems a little too bold or a little too weak, pick the bolder version. Its strength will diminish when it covers the walls—the more you have of something, the less you see of it.

Tape large wallpaper samples up on the wall and live with these choices for a few days before making up your mind. Test them under daylight and nighttime conditions for a more accurate reading.

The Enriching Qualities of Fabric

Fabric adds color and texture to walls, with or without the additional element of pattern. It can heighten the elegance of a setting if the fabric in question is silk or silklike, or accentuate the room's easy informality with a rough-hewn texture. Whatever the choice, fabric adds enrichment whether applied flat or shirred. The latter is not as impractical as it may first sound, as the shirred fabric can be installed from rod to rod (from ceiling or crown molding to baseboard) and then removed for cleaning. This approach is extremely decorative; professionals favor it occasionally for bedroom or dining-room decoration. The walls themselves need no preparation; shirred fabric immediately camouflages a multitude of sins. (Sheathing walls with fabric is a complicated task, and should not be attempted by an amateur.)

The recent popularity of laminated wall coverings—fabric or textures such as burlap or grasscloth attached to a paper backing—derives from the fact that these laminates offer the ease of wallpaper installation with the added dimension of a textured surface. Laminates are also made with wood grains, leatherlike and other textures that require little if any maintenance and promise long wear and durability.

In addition to being painted a different color from the walls, ceilings can also be dramatized by inventive decorating techniques. A striped wallpaper or fabric print can be mitered for a tent effect; fabric can also add textural interest when applied in the spaces between ceiling beams. So can a lively pattern that relates to the colors of the room or matches the pattern be used for pillows or an upholstered design.

Beams and wall shelf in natural pine were added to the wall of a small sitting room to give it additional architectural interest. The common denominator of informality ties together a mix of disparate furnishings, including peacock chair, wicker chest used as a table, assorted framed prints, and canvas and wood chair and bench. Sisal matting covers the floor.

Add-on molding and a rich and warm color scheme of rose, pink, mauve, and olive give an ingratiating hospitality to a room filled with Early American favorites. Note surprising but compatible elements such as jabots used with narrow blinds, the dhurrie rug. Room designed by Margot Gunther.

Mirrors

An expensive background element, but a superb space expander, mirror is still another material often used for walls and ceilings. Even a narrow wall of mirror will go a long way to visually multiply space as well as invest a room with enormous vitality and sparkle. There is nothing more dramatic than a room filled with bold colors and mirrored walls.

BATH AND FIXTURES BY SHERLE WAGNER INTERNATIONAL

Mirrored closet doors add to the sparkle and the illusion of endless space in a bathroom design by Audrey Zauderer. Pretty floral wall covering, and matching fabric and rug, give a fresh and pastoral flavor to a room of generous proportions. Bathtub is sheathed with marble, and marble also makes the floor tiles, while simple vertical blinds give a sleek look to the windows.

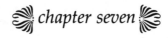

chapter seven

Window Treatments

Beautifully dressed windows enrich the style and character of an interior, yet they should never be thought of as "frosting on the cake" but rather as a basic element of background decoration and an integral part of the overall design scheme.

And more important, windows must be permitted to serve their primary roles: to let in light and air rather than to be decorated for decoration's sake. Of course a window serves still another role during nighttime hours, but the treatment of a window must accommodate each of these roles. It hardly makes sense to install a handsome window treatment, even one that works beautifully with the style of the room, if it totally obscures a magnificent view or affords little flexibility in light and privacy control.

Skillful window dressing can accomplish many things. It can emphasize rich architectural detail, erase an ugly view, "correct" off-balance wall proportions, enlarge an undersized window, provide the softening effect of fabric or the hard-edged sleekness of narrow blinds. Window treatments also provide noise and weather insulation.

Because window treatment is not only a very powerful decorating tool but a three-dimensional one as well, the process may appear to be a very complex one to the amateur. How does one narrow down the choices to come up with the most appropriate and attractive solution?

Use a Common-sense Approach

The best approach is a common-sense one rather than a super-scientific one and should be based on these general principles: Gear the window treatment to the type and limitations of the window style, to the role or roles the window must play, and to the style mood of the furnishings within the room. Color must also relate. The fabric or material chosen for the window treatment can either match the walls, repeat a texture chosen for a major upholstered piece, or reiterate one of the accent colors in the room.

As you go along, you will discover that there will be more than one possible solution to each of your window-dressing needs. Try to be a little flexible here. If your furniture plan calls for positioning a piece in front of the window, you might replace one window-dressing concept for another. Remember, also, that your budget and practical requirements may also set limits on the kinds of window treatments you can choose. The more elaborate, usually the more costly, are harder to maintain.

Types of Windows

Double Hung: The garden-variety window with two panels or sashes that move up or down, so that the window can be opened at the top or at the bottom. Such windows lend themselves to a number of possible treatments, precluding, however, an approach such as vertical blinds, which would make the opening of double-hung windows an awkward affair.

Casement: A combination of stationary panels or panes with a door that opens in or out of the room. A window treatment must leave room enough for the protruding handles of the casement doors. If a casement door swings into the room that also must be taken into consideration when the window treatment is selected.

Picture Window and Window Wall: A popular approach to window architecture since the end of World War II. Designed primarily to fully expose a great view, the concept is often abused and used for rooms that face a dreary landscape or a brick wall, for that matter. The amateur tends toward the wall-to-wall look for window walls, overpowering a room with yards and yards of billowy fabric. Try to let a certain amount of wall frame the window; if the view is that great, consider no treatment at all.

French Doors: A handsome architectural *tour de force* that are actually windowed doors. If they open into the room, you will be limited in choice, as they can interfere with a full drapery treatment. Fabric shirred on poles set within the top and bottom of the window frame is often a good solution here. Another is laminated shades.

Bay Window: A window set within a recess, or a three-sided projection (when viewed from outside the house). Can be given a single integrating window dressing or three individual ones, such as Roman shades, or shutters.

Jalousies: These are also called louvered windows and are composed of many horizontal slats of glass that can be manipulated so that the entire area can be opened up.

Bow Window: A curved version of a bay window.

Sliding Glass Doors: A product of modern architecture, they afford easy accessibility to garden or terrace. Provide a treatment that does not block the passageway but still softens or covers the large black rectangle that such doors become at night.

Dormer Windows: Usually small windows set within the recess of a sloping roof. The narrowness of the area calls for a treatment that blends the windows in with the walls.

Ranch or Strip Windows: Once a popular style during the period of ranch-house design, these pose certain decorating problems as they are shallow and placed high on the wall.

Other less common window types include clerestories (shallow windows set near the ceiling, above a door, or in a gable), cathedral windows (windows that extend the full height of a two-story living room), arched windows, skylights, and horizontally sliding windows.

Window Treatment Design

Window treatments break down into two basic categories: soft treatments (those made almost exclusively from fabric such as curtains and draperies) and hard treatments (those made from stiff materials such as wood shutters, metal blinds). Often the prescribed window dressing is a combination of two treatments, such as draperies used in tandem with curtains, shades, or blinds, or shutters paired with shades. Sometimes two are used for a special decorative effect because one alone would not provide sufficient light or privacy control.

Draperies: These can hang straight or be tied back, and are one of the most popular window treatments due to their versatility. Lined and interlined, they can supply noise and temperature insulation. Pulled back, they reveal a view; closed, they shut off the black of night. Draperies can be pinch-pleated and hung from a traverse rod or shirred on a pole. The kind of fabric chosen, silk as compared to linen, velvet in contrast to cotton duck, will determine the degree of formality or informality. So will the addition of trimming such as tape, tassels, and fringe. These latter are usually used for drapery treatments in a primarily traditional room. Draperies are almost always floor length.

Curtains: Curtains are used alone as an underpinning for tie-back draperies. To filter daylight, they are made of sheer or casement fabrics. The popular cafe curtain is a short design, often covering only the lower half of a double-hung window, but used primarily in a two-tier effect. They can be suspended from a rod by wooden rings or self loops. When curtains are combined with draperies, one or both can be stationary. Permanent drapery panels give a finished look to a large window covered with sheer curtains that can be pulled back to reveal a view. Or both the curtains and draperies can be installed, close to each other, on traverse rods so that one or both can be opened or closed or partially closed.

Swags and Jabots: The kind of window treatment often used in eighteenth-century English and American rooms. A length of fabric is pulled in a curved or swag shape and gathered at each corner of the window frame top. The fabric that hangs down is called the jabot. This kind of treatment can be used alone or as a topping for tie-back

Small windows are made large and beautiful by the addition of tie-back curtains with double-shirred tops that achieve a valance effect. Skillful furniture selection and placement maximizes space in a modest-sized living room whose bright colorings of pink and brick are stated in easy-care durable Herculon fabrics. Note accents of natural materials, such as bamboo blinds, wicker look on tables and étagère, basket accessories,

draperies. It was often a popular choice for small mullioned windows of Colonial homes; used alone, it permitted the deep, paneled reveals (window recesses) to be seen.

Window Shades: These come in assorted variations ranging from the light-screening pull-down shade to the more elaborate Roman and Austrian styles. The basic, pull-down roller shade is no longer your Plain Jane window treatment and now comes in many different textures, a rainbow choice of colors, can be hand-painted, stenciled, even laminated with a fabric used for draperies or for upholstery. They can even be given the further embellishment of appliqués or fringes. Unless installed reverse-roll (so that the roller is not seen), the top of the shade should be covered by a cornice or valance. Roman shades are flat when completely lowered, but when pulled up, these fabric shades fold into pleats for a trim, tailored look that can blend with any style decor. For this reason, Roman shades are made of heavy fabric and are lined. While a single roll-up window shade can make three small adjacent windows look like one large one, Roman shades can also provide a decorative way of subdividing a large window wall if one is attempting to provide period furnishings with a more traditional background treatment. Laminated pull-up shades and matching lambrequins are still another way of giving traditional character to stark windows. Austrian shades, similar in principle to Roman shades, have deeply draped swags, top to bottom, and are usually fashioned from elegant materials and used in very formal interiors.

Matchstick Blinds: These have become a popular choice of professional designers because they are unobtrusive yet provide textural interest, combine readily with overdraperies, and can be used in rooms with varying degrees of formality or informality. These roll up, as do their heavier versions, the bamboo blinds. The somewhat open quality of these woven blinds permits a certain amount of light to filter through, so they can be used as another alternative to sheer curtains.

Venetian Blinds: In recent years, Venetian blinds are being favored in a much narrower version of what was originally a blind of wide wooden or metal slats, which could be completely or partially opened, depending upon the degree of light desired. They're a popular choice for rooms of modern architecture and modern furnishings as well as for interiors of limited space. Their sleek appearance does not eat up space visually, as a fuller, fabric window treatment would tend to do. Today Venetian blinds are available in an extraordinary variety of colors and textures; they can even be ordered in striped effects. Their light control potential has an enormous range.

Vertical Blinds: A vertical version of the Venetian blind, with slats running vertically rather than horizontally. While slats are usually wider, these blinds also offer superb refinement in light control and are another excellent choice for contemporary rooms. They are made of metal or of fabric, and as they hang from ceiling tracks to the floor, they can be used to transform badly proportioned windows and to enlarge small ones. More architectural than decorative, vertical blinds are an excellent choice for window walls and interiors with a sophisticated ambiance.

Shutters: An abiding favorite, wood shutters flourish inside the home as well as outside it. In stained finishes they proffer the warmth of wood and an enriching architectural accent. Or painted the color of the window frame, they can serve as a trim and versatile background element, accommodating both traditional and contemporary decor. Traditional shutters are made with movable louvers or slats that can be adjusted according to the amount of light required. Other shutter styles include those with frames of wood draped with shirred fabric or inset with fabric-covered panels. An entire window can be filled with a complement of shutters; one or two pairs can frame a window of curtains.

Cornices and Valances: These give architectural focus and a finishing framework to draperies and curtains. A cornice can be made of wood, painted or stained, or can be upholstered and covered with a fabric that matches the fabric of walls and/or draperies. It hides curtain heading and hardware, and usually extends the window about four or so inches in depth. Cornices can be straight-lined or they can have decorative shaping. Valances are either swagged or pleated; they are a softer version of the cornice, do not have a plywood base, but effectively serve the same purpose.

Lambrequins: Similar to a cornice in shape and stiffness, but more extensive, framing the window on all three sides. Here's an easy way to supply a needed architectural element, enlarge a small window, make the windows a more powerful ingredient in the decorating scheme. Like cornices, lambrequins are often upholstered in the same fabric used for curtains or a shade set within the frame.

Other Window Treatments: We have covered the basic, most often used window treatment approaches and styles. Of course there are other, less frequently employed, sometimes exotic treatments that are occasionally chosen by designers to create a specific look, provide an unusual decorative accent. These include sliding shoji panels and fretwork screening, tall folding panels, a pair of antique or fabric-covered screens, free-standing at each end of a window, column or panel dividers, which break up a window wall, pull-up shades, often used in concert with the pull-down kind, swing-out curtains that provide softening yet do not obstruct a great view, double tie-backs, shiny metal blinds—to name a few.

The fabric chosen for any of the window treatments that require it must be part of the total fabric "package" of the room, not an isolated selection. As such it will be consistent with the tone or mood of the room and will not feature an unexpected or inappropriate pattern or texture. Window fabric selection should be worked out when the entire fabric plan of the room is being developed. More will be said on this in our chapter on fabric selection. If a fabric used for upholstery is to be repeated at the windows, the question often is "Which one?" Here, other considerations should come into play. For insulation, a heavier texture should be chosen; for less density, a sheerer quality. It is often desirable to continue a print at the window that has been used on one or two pieces of upholstery—to bring a balance of pattern into the total composition. Fabrics that match the wallpaper create spatial continuity when repeated for draperies or curtains. The choice of fabric and the amount of trimming used will of course determine to what degree a window treatment will seem traditional or even period pure. More simple interpretations tend to appear more contemporary; these are often preferred for rooms with mixed furnishings, with an eclectic style mood.

Windows with a Great View

When the view from a window is fabulous both day and night, such as that from a window wall of a city apartment on a high floor, the window can be left completely bare, so that the view becomes a real part of the room's decorative interest. If desired, some framing can be used, perhaps stationary draperies or panels. And there are ways to break up the long expanse of a window that lacks a pleasing view other than the typical curtain wall. A series of tie-back draperies can be installed; so can a row of arch-shaped lambrequins, or a series of fabric-covered or mirrored panels, or beams, installed at regular intervals.

While a simple pair of curtains can be whipped up in minutes on the machine, even by a beginner, it takes enormous precision and expertise to handle the more complicated varieties of window dressing. These should usually be entrusted to workrooms and drapery shops that specialize in custom design. Of course labor is expensive, so limit your use of extensive drapery work if you do not intend to stay put. Or if your budget is small. Allocate the money sensibly; don't go overboard on backgrounds or window treatments. Often you can temporize, by first buying blinds or curtains for light control and privacy, adding overdraperies at a later date when you can more easily afford them. If your decorating plan calls for draperies that match the wallpaper or the sofa cover, it would be practical to order the required yardage at the same time in case the fabric is discontinued or comes in different dye lots.

Budgeting the Drapery Dollar

A further word about budgeting: Don't try to stretch your drapery dollar by skimping on yardage. Draperies should be very full and sheer curtains at least three times their width; both should be made with deep hems for a quality look. A much more viable way to save is with stock ready-mades, which are available today in a staggering variety of textures, patterns, and sizes. You can always add fringe, tape, braid, and gimp to make any of these store-bought window dressings look richer, even custom-made.

Hardware is the hidden element in any window treatment installation. These include traverse and straight or unadjustable rods, brackets, poles, rings, metal tie-backs, hooks, and these will determine the amount of movement of your window design—the pulling back and forth together of draperies and curtains. Hardware should almost always be concealed, except when it is part of the decorative style, such as poles and rings. Be sure that your hardware is properly installed to ensure symmetry at your windows.

While you should try to avoid overly elaborate, "fancy-schmancy" window treatments, don't be overly conservative. Window design is a creative decorating tool that if used with taste and imagination can augment the personal style of your interior, and can provide a large measure of its charm.

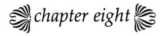 *chapter eight*

Fabrics

For many people, shopping for fabrics is one of the most pleasurable phases of the decorating game. What appears to be a limitless array of fabric samples on view in fabric showrooms or departments present, in their own way, as great a feast for the eye as paintings in a museum. Each new pattern or texture seems more delicious than the last, and one is likely to come away with far more samples and far more possible combinations than can actually be used.

To simplify the procedure, one should never shop for fabrics "blind," or without some basic plan, some fairly specific idea of what to look for. This can be done only after one has first mapped out the fabric strategy for each and every room. Will the fabrics all be in smooth or textured weaves or is the scheme a combination of correlated patterns? Does the mood of the decor call for elegant textures or informal, casual materials? Is the drapery fabric to match the wall color or the sofa print? Does the role of the room preclude the use of fragile textures and colors? Is the decorating style traditional, modern, or mixed? Will most of the pattern go on the larger upholstered designs or be used primarily for accent?

These, plus other considerations such as climate and personal taste, will also help to define your fabric choices. If you have not as yet worked out a color scheme but expect to base it on whatever fabric print is chosen for sofa and draperies, then of course you will first have to search out such a print and use it as your starting point.

Sometimes, by going out in the market, you will find fabrics that suggest a more interesting solution than your original plan or suggest some possible minor modifications. Fabric selection is a dynamic procedure; what you find may alter to a major or minor degree the original concept for your room.

Pattern

Pattern provides an almost foolproof way of providing a room with zest, with strong decorative interest. Expressed in regal damasks or country calicoes, patterned fabrics can wake up a room with dreary architecture, give style to pedestrian furniture designs, integrate a mixed collection of furnishings. What kind of pattern should be used, and to what degree, will be determined by the type of room you are decorating, as well as by its style mood. You might use oodles of a single pattern in a young lady's bedroom, but limit your pattern choice to pillows and draperies in a living room. Other patterned elements to be chosen for the room—rugs, wallpaper, paintings—will also determine the amount of pattern required or wanted for fabrics.

Patterned fabrics are either woven or printed, and are offered in a superb choice of styles, ranging from authentic documentaries and crewels to provincial plaids and florals and modern geometrics. If you are planning to use a pattern, the basic furniture design of the room should supply some direction. But if you are seeking to contemporize your room when you reupholster, you might consider replacing a period toile with a free-wheeling floral or enlivening solid textures with a few small-scale geometrics.

Bold Patterns for Certain Areas

As with bold color, strong pattern is usually limited to rooms that get less living use, such as dining rooms, bedrooms, entries. Such patterns are not as flexible as plain textures; one tends to tire of them more quickly. In allocating pattern to a room, try to ensure some kind of balance. Avoid using the same print as the draperies on chairs near the window—it throws too much pattern over to one side of the room. Instead, repeat the print on a sofa that's nearer to the wall opposite the windows.

A medley of patterns and lively colors can prevent a supersized living room from looking empty or cold. Designer Robert Metzger used this approach most successfully in this romantically buoyant living room, which blends period furniture with contemporary paintings. Copious storage is offered by decorative wall units.

Designers occasionally concentrate pattern with pattern for a provocative look, a dramatic interplay. Actually it's not a new idea; period rooms were often executed in a mix of three patterns or even more. Fabric manufacturers have made it very easy for us to apply this look by creating correlated collections, groups of two or more patterns that are color and design coordinated. Usually one of the designs is large-scale; the others are smaller or else linear interpretations such as checks and plaids. Working within such a collection, rather than trying to coordinate on your own, leaves much less room for error.

Don't jump from one pattern style to a totally different one for rooms that adjoin each other. Follow the same principles that you would use in the application of color. Adjacent rooms should relate, not look jarringly different from each other.

Most patterns come in a choice of colors; these are called "color ways." You will discover that the same pattern, whether a print or a woven design, projects a totally different look in each of its color ways. The combination of colors can determine the liveliness of the pattern; obviously a mix of bold hues will give the pattern much more verve than a blend of neutrals. Traditional color will make a documentary print seem more authentic than if a contemporary color is used.

Color and Scale Variations

Patterns can change their personality according to the other colors used for the room. Vibrant colors can intensify the power of a print, while subtle colors will tone it down.

Be careful of scale. Large patterns can overpower beautiful furnishings. Tiny patterns that seem appropriate in sample form can wash out when used on large surfaces such as a long sofa.

Patterns that combine three or more colors look very different from a distance than they do up close. Sometimes totally new colors emerge as the eye "mixes" the colors involved. Adjacent reds and blues, for example, could blur together for a purplish tone. So if you want to co-ordinate the pattern with matching plains, get a "distance reading," don't exact-match the plains to the separate colors in the pattern. Patterns also shape up differently when utilized for full draperies, so hold a sample in folds to get the right effect.

There's no formula that says you have to repeat the pattern chosen for draperies on some of the upholstered furniture. The same chintz used at the windows could also make a skirted table and some big throw pillows for the sofa.

Texture

Pattern supplies a room with personality; texture establishes its mood. A setting filled with silken damasks evokes a totally different mood from one styled with nubby tweeds. Textured fabrics can reinforce the style of the furniture or play it down.

All the "plain" fabrics that are chosen for a room have some kind of texture, running the gamut from shiny smooth silks and cotton chintzes to rough-hewn homespuns. And while texture is a much more subtle element than pattern, it can be employed just as effectively to create decorative interest and diversity.

In a monochromatic scheme, for example, a counterpoint of contrasting textures, all expressed in similar colors, can generate visual as well as tactile interest. But when textures are combined with powerful pattern, it's wise to cut down on textural variety in order to avoid a busy look.

Even a beginner knows the difference between a formal, elegant fabric and a casual, easygoing texture merely by looking at them. The style of furniture you are using should position your choices, but even here there is room for a certain amount of flexibility. You may wish to accentuate the handcrafted look of country pieces by finding fabrics that are handwoven or have a homespun look. Or you can go the other way with smoother sailcloths and ducks. Cover seating modules with a slubbed texture, they take on one appearance; with a mellow velvet, they become something else.

Certain textures tend to be identified as "feminine" or "masculine." Embroidered fabrics, taffetas, satins, and antique velvets fall into the first category; leathers, tweeds, corduroys, and felts into the second. Of course certain patterns can be described in the same way, such as delicate florals vis-à-vis large-scale plaids. So if you are aiming for a very precise look—for a man's den or a woman's bedroom—it's a good idea to keep these distinctions in mind. Leather, or leather-look vinyl, mixed with plaids and tweeds instantly conveys the no-nonsense, casual style so right for a man's hideaway. Here a concentration of "masculine" textures and patterns reinforces the mood already set by informal furniture designs.

Textures drape according to tightness of weave and fiber content. The lighter, thinner weaves produce a softer, more billowy drapery; heavier textures create a bulkier, stiffer effect. Polished finishes, such as that used for chintz, produce a crisper look than softer, open-weave casement cloths.

If you are purchasing your fabrics at a reliable store, they will be able to tell you just what to expect in terms of wear, soil-resistance, color fading, etc., from any fabric you might buy. Fiber blends will of course offer you the combined advantages and limitations of the individual fibers. When soiling is a potential problem, especially for white or pale fabrics, soil-resistant finishes can be applied at an extra charge that is well worth the money. Many manufacturers automatically use such finishes in fabric production. The label identifies the finish, if any has been used.

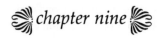
chapter nine

Floor Coverings

Pattern, color, texture underfoot—floor coverings provide all three. They can be purely decorative or supply needed insulation; they can expand a room visually or provide the precise punctuation of pattern. They can camouflage and renew, inject a sea of bold color or texture.

Choosing the right floor covering for each room involves a number of considerations. You don't just decide that you want wall-to-wall carpeting and then go out and buy it. Your floor treatment has to tie in with the style scheme of the room, must work with the furniture arrangement, harmonize with fabric patterns and textures. Traffic lanes and heavy wear are still other considerations.

First you must assess the floor with which you are dealing. If it's a beautiful wood parquet, in excellent condition, can you leave it bare or use only one or two accent rugs? You might choose not to cover it in a dining area but add a large area carpet for comfort in a living room. If the floor is stained, cracked, and ugly, then wall-to-wall carpeting will probably be the most logical choice. If so, what color, texture, and price?

The kind of room—living room, dining room, kitchen, etc.,—and the style of the room will have a great deal to do with your floor-covering selection. Chances are that you'll want a fully carpeted floor in the bedroom and, perhaps, ceramic tile in a garden room. Ease of care and durability will be more significant in some rooms than in others.

When you are assembling your samples for wallpaper, paint, and fabrics, you must also be working on the floor treatment. The selections must all be interrelated; what fabrics are used will influence the choice of floor covering, and vice versa.

Area Rugs

Let's say, for example, that you want to use a large area rug but favor a fair amount of pattern in your upholstery and drapery fabrics. Then the area rug should be one solid color, or at most have a simple border design. If the mix of patterns is of small-scale provincials, this does not preclude your choosing a braided rug in correlated colors, as these kinds of fabric and rug patterns tend to blend easily.

Area rugs over smooth floors is a more interesting kind of treatment than the somewhat anonymous wall-to-wall look. It's not only more personal, it serves an architectural role as well by integrating or unifying a furniture grouping, by separating the larger living area from the dining ell or alcove, by visually altering the superlong or huge, barnlike proportions of a room. Area rugs can play the most provocative part in the stage setting by supplying the only powerful pattern in a room with plain fabrics.

Once available only in expensive custom designs, area rugs are now made in every kind of fiber, texture, pattern, and price range; marvelous motifs and colors are no longer the prerogative of the few.

Many area rugs are interpreted in monochromatic "carved look," patterns, those shaped in precise levels of pile. Such rugs are as versatile as wall-to-wall carpeting but are more architectural and can be turned clockwise to avoid the excessive soiling and wear marks of an entrenched traffic lane. And of course they can be more easily sent out for cleaning at less expense.

Patterned area rugs are inspired by designs from all corners of the globe, are sometimes frankly new, boldly modern interpretations, and just as often, fresh, updated versions of traditional favorites. And they're not just rectangular anymore, but come in free-form, oval, hexagonal, even octagonal shapes.

Area rug patterns run the gamut from charming provincial styles, modern geometrics and abstracts, large-scale florals, primitive and ethnic patterns, and bold plaids to plain textures with striped or patterned borders. Furlike rugs, such as the Flokatis from Greece as well as those of real fur, such as sheepskin, alpaca, and steerhide, supply the sumptuous kind of texture often needed to soften hard-edge furnishings.

Oriental Rugs

Imports from all over the world—needlepoints from France and Portugal, deeply textured Moroccan designs, ryas from Sweden—offer great textural diversity. Flat weaves have become a favorite choice of designers in recent years—dhurries from India, Kelims from the Middle East, and the ever-popular Navajo rug made by the American Indian or by machine. Many of these imported styles are expensive, but savings on installation, which would be necessary for wall-to-wall, might make these an affordable solution.

Oriental rugs deserve to be reckoned with as a special category of area rug design, as they encompass a broad range of styles. They are also extremely versatile and can be used in rooms of just about any decorative style. Most of those orientals imported from China, Turkey, Pakistan, India, Japan, and Iran (Persia) are hand-knotted, but less costly machine-made orientals are also available, though much less impressive.

A study of all the oriental designs extant would be extensive enough to fill a college course. As with buying wine, you don't have to fully understand the genre to know whether you like it or not. Many oriental rugs have all-over motifs, while others feature center medallions. The latter are somewhat more difficult to use because the medallion should be centered in the furniture grouping for a balanced effect.

A beautiful oriental rug is like a painting on the floor, and while expensive, it is also an excellent investment, as such rugs are becoming shorter and shorter in supply. They're very practical too, as they are durable and don't show soil or footmarks. They can be found in an enormous range of sizes that go way beyond the usual stock dimensions. The more tightly woven the oriental, the longer lasting and the more costly—but the value is greater. As orientals age, they take on a patina that even intensifies their beauty, which is why so many worn, "semiantique" orientals appreciate in value over the years. Most oriental rugs are made with decorative fringes.

Carpeting and Room-size Rugs

Wall-to-wall carpeting is wide-width or broadloom (usually twelve-foot) that has been cut out to totally cover all the existing floor area in a room. It is tacked down over a padding, unless it has a self-cushion. This is a much more permanent installation than a room-size rug, which usually permits a certain amount of border to show around its perimeter. But there is a substantial amount of waste involved in cutting carpeting so that it completely covers a given floor.

While area rugs can add bold decorative interest, mark off areas of activity, frame a dining arrangement, or lighten a dark corner, carpeting provides warmth underfoot, an integrating flow of color, a buffer to noisy footsteps or neighbors. It can proffer a sweep of vibrant color or impart the softening strokes of subtle hues. Deeply rich carpet tones can balance the finishes of dark woods; matching carpeting can complete a monochromatic scheme. Carpeting can go up the walls to insulate, or cover raised seating levels, or upholster a bed platform.

Depending upon construction and finishing techniques, carpeting can be rough-hewn shag or plush velvet, can have a tightly woven twist texture or a surface of level loops. It can be random sheared, feature very high or very low pile. Density of weave, fiber content, and height of pile affects its style as well as its price and wear potential.

It's a safe rule of thumb to say that the shaggier a carpet's texture, the greater its affinity for informal, tailored rooms. Plush velvets, on the other hand, sustain the sense of luxe in elegant settings.

Once, wall-to-wall carpeting was installed, indiscriminately, as the ultimate status symbol. Today it should be used only when it is the best solution. Chopped up, tiny apartments benefit from its integrating sweep of color and texture; badly marred wood floors are instantly renewed. It's a favorite choice for bedrooms, supplying a warming accent and the softness of texture under bare feet.

Since wall-to-wall carpeting cannot be rotated, avoid fragile colors in rooms that get hard wear. They'll quickly show soil and traffic patterns. Dense and tightly twisted pile is a fine choice for heavy-duty rooms.

At one time, all carpeting was made of wool and manufactured on high-investment looms. Today, the innovations of modern technology, such as tufting, printing, cross-dyeing, and the development of synthetic fibers and new backings, have brought what once was a luxury product within the reach of many.

Some understanding of the various fibers available and their special properties will give you additional guidelines to help you make the right choice.

Wool: Extremely resilient, with great natural warmth, less likely to crush, long-wearing and flame-resistant. Requires skillful professional cleaning, mothproofing, and does not come through with as much color clarity as most synthetics. An inexpensive wool carpet is not a good value because wool should be fairly dense to provide its advantages.

Nylon: Just about the strongest, best-wearing synthetic around, nylon accounts for an enormous percentage of carpet production. Dyes beautifully and retains color. Resists soil and stains, conceals dirt, and has good resiliency. A certain amount of static buildup is likely with nylon textures, but this can be minimized by certain additives. Sheen varies according to the manufacturer.

Acrylics: Feels and looks very much like wool, but much stronger ounce for ounce. Excellent cleanability, soil resistance, color clarity, and springiness. Resistant to mildew and moths, as are most other synthetics. Nonallergenic, but there may be some pilling.

Polyesters: Since the polyester fiber is bulky, carpets made from it are very luxurious in texture for the money—only a little more costly than nylon. Resists most stains except oil-based ones and is mildew, moth, and allergy resistant with little static buildup or pilling. Offers great textural diversity, fine color range.

Olefins: The popular indoor-outdoor carpet fiber that goes out into the patio or covers the kitchen floor. Ease of cleaning and moisture resistance as well as good durability make it an excellent choice for such heavy-duty areas or the outdoors.

Modified Acrylics and Rayons: Also used for floor coverings, these are primarily for bath and scatter rugs. Rayon is a good blending fiber and inexpensive with only fair soil- and crush-resistant properties but extremely easy to clean.

How long you expect to stay in your present home and how much wear the carpet will receive should serve to guide your choice of quality and price. Of course wall-to-wall carpeting can always be picked up and installed in a room of equal or smaller dimensions. Or cut into a room-size or accent rug.

For a special look you can give a wall-to-wall installation an inlaid border, which can mark off the bed arrangement or a furniture grouping much the way an area rug does. Or a geometrically patterned carpet can be inset within the larger framework of a solid wall-to-wall carpeting, again for an area rug look, with the convenience and comfort of a completely covered floor.

Be sure to buy your carpeting and rugs at a reliable store, one that will stand behind its merchandise, that will sell you the quality that is appropriate, not only in pile density, but in padding—which you will need for rugs as well as for wall-to-wall installations.

Smooth Surface Flooring

When wall-to-wall carpeting was *the* way to keep up with the Joneses, even the most beautiful parquet floors were hidden under a spread of deep texture. Today, happily, we are free to make the most of smooth flooring as a superb alternative to carpets and rugs. We may choose a smooth material because we like the way it looks and the ways in which it works with our design scheme. And/or because of certain practical merits.

Plush carpeting is not the only route to elegance; a highly polished floor of herringbone parquet, a gleaming cover of black vinyl or white ceramic tile can each contribute a different and unique kind of luxury. Nor are shaggy textures the only way to informality; quarry tile, brick, and slate are wonderful anchors for a casual room.

Actually, smooth and textured floor coverings are often used in concert; this counterpoint of materials adds enrichment to the decorative impact of the room and usually makes it more comfortable and versatile as well. Whether you choose one or both will depend upon the kind of room with which you are dealing. Small areas that get lots of hard wear, such as a foyer or entry hall, are excellent candidates for a smooth floor. So is a dining room, where the spilling of food and drink is a constant maintenance problem. Family rooms that are adjacent to the outdoors and are given hard wear by teen-agers and parents, when they entertain informally, are another fine place for a floor that mops clean.

Sometimes it's simply a matter of improving what you already have

—such as refinishing a stained but still beautiful wood floor. In other instances, you may want or need to put a new floor down. Again, as we have suggested in the choice of carpeting, work out your flooring selections in relation to fabric, furniture, and color-scheme choices.

Don't make the floor an afterthought or install it on impulse just because you like it but have no real ideas, as yet, how the area will be furnished. A rug, of course, can be added later, or just put down during the winter months if some warming accent is needed when the winds are blowing. Be sensible with your budget, too. While it's prudent to purchase a quality product rather than trying to stint, don't spend so much on the floor that you have little left over for the rest of the furnishings. It pays to wait; if you can't afford what you want, temporize with a carpet of sisal, a "natural"-look material that provides cover and adds style, too.

Here's a general outline of the smooth materials available:

Wood: Its abiding beauty has made it a favored choice over the centuries. Can be elegant parquet, casual random planking, or the commonly used tongue-and-groove strip flooring. The cost of wood flooring is predicated on perfection of graining rather than durability, so if you are furnishing an informal room, choose one of the lesser grades. It will be just as long-wearing but more rustic and better suited to your decor. Oak and maple are the most popular woods for flooring, but teak, walnut, beech, birch, and pecan are also used. Manufacturers now offer wood in tiles, and wood flooring that has been commercially finished.

Ordinary wood floors can be transformed into colorful and highly decorative spaces by the application of heavy-duty enamel floor paint to create vivid stretches of a single color. Freely painted or stenciled designs can invest such floors with any pattern or look imaginable. Coats of polyurethane, added after the paint has dried, ensures longer wear and ease of cleaning. Unpainted wood floors should be waxed and buffed whenever the eye deems it necessary.

Ceramic Tile: Currently a very popular choice for dens, family rooms, sun rooms, kitchens, activity rooms, and foyers because of enormous variety of color offered, ease of maintenance, extreme durability. Not as resilient as wood or the vinyl synthetics. Simply needs to be mopped clean.

Slate and Brick: These rugged natural materials are often used in modern interiors for their specific textural qualities; in recent seasons they have emerged as popular flavorings for rough-hewn country rooms. Easy to care for and durable, but expensive to install and not resilient. Recommended for small areas, or wherever their unique character is desired.

Marble: The quintessential luxury smooth surface, associated with the palaces of yesteryear, still used for foyers, bathrooms, and other areas when the budget permits. Does not need waxing but stains easily.

Rubber: Once a very popular flooring (before the advent of vinyl), rubber has great resiliency, hence dents are only temporary. Rubber stains readily.

Resilient Flooring

Whatever smooth surface material you choose, be sure to consider its resiliency or lack of it. Such a quality is underfoot for floors on which you may stand for periods of time—as in a kitchen or work center. When a flooring serves a purely decorative purpose, this is no longer a factor.

Vinyl: Available in sheeting or in tile sizes. This relatively new (about thirty years old) synthetic product has enormously broadened the range of texture and color variety of smooth flooring. Now used where once linoleum held sway—kitchens, playrooms, family rooms, basements—vinyl is often elegant enough for an entrance hall or dining room, depending upon quality, finish, color, and texture. Comes in its own textures as well as imitiations of such natural materials as wood graining and parquet, brick, cork, marble, terrazzo, and ceramic. Inlaid patterned vinyl sheeting is offered in a staggering choice of designs, and is highly durable as the pattern is built all the way through the material. Vinyl sheeting is also offered with its own cushioned backing for greater resilience; many vinyl tiles are now made for easy do-it-yourself installation.

Asphalt Tile: Inexpensive and porous, it is a fine choice for on-grade (cement, for example) installations, requires a certain amount of maintenance, will show dents easily, and does not absorb noise.

Vinyl-Asbestos: Another good choice for on-grade installation as it is low in price, easy to put down, durable, and easily cleaned. It is dent- and stain-resistant, but does not absorb noise and is not resilient.

Cork: Has a unique texture and superb resilience and is a wonderful noise insulator, but stains readily and requires skillful installation.

Terrazzo: A composite of stone or marble chips, very durable and easy to clean.

There are many interesting things that one can do to create a very personal and unusual floor design. A patterned area "rug" can be produced with stenciled designs and a painted border; a large-scale vinyl tile can be installed with wood-look stripping for the effect of a custom floor. Bleaching and tinting can provide a plain wood floor with unexpected elegance and a light touch. Another smooth-surface area-rug idea: a bordered pattern inlayed within a vinyl floor.

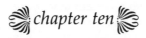 *chapter ten*

Furniture—
What to Choose

Constructing a furniture-plan or room-arrangement scheme, and then finding in the marketplace those furniture designs that will turn this plan into reality, is one of the most challenging as well as the most rewarding phases of any interior design project.

Almost everything else that goes into a room is some form of embellishment; it is the furniture that makes an interior work, that makes it serve its primary (and secondary) roles—e.g., sleeping, living, sitting, study, dining. No matter what its style, furniture is functional; it provides a place to sit on, or to lie on, a surface to hold plates and glasses, interior areas to store clothing and household possessions. Even the most ornamental furniture design serves some basic purpose as well as a decorative one.

It is never enough, therefore, merely to settle on a furniture style and then to assign to each room the usual complement of furniture. For there is no usual complement. Your own needs and life-style requirements, the size of the room and its architecture, are variables that will determine to a large extent how much upholstery you will buy, whether you will use many tables or just a few, a mix of finishes or a matched look. Is all your furniture to be made of wood or are some metal accents a possibility?

Sort Out Your Options

Of course your furniture arrangement plan will finalize these decisions. But you cannot make an intelligent floor plan unless you first know what all the options are and have sorted them out. Obviously, there are certain "musts" for each room—a table for the dining area, a bed for the bedroom—but there is usually a certain amount of space left over for optionals. These choices do not have to be frozen into the plan; you can do a certain amount of changing and modifying as you go along, as you discover on your shopping tours some unanticipated possibilities.

You may decide, after some heavy shopping, that you would really prefer to use a series of seating modules instead of a pair of sofas. This may require some radical changing around in the floor plan, but don't hesitate to do it, even if you have to work out the new plan from scratch. Decorating is a learning experience; in the shopping and browsing rather than buying phase of furniture selection you can enjoy the luxury of changing your mind.

It is only by becoming familiar with what is offered that one can pare down the choices, assess them judiciously, and create an interior that pleases the eye and comforts the family. So let us systematically review the entire spectrum of furniture choice, breaking it down into upholstery and case goods (tables, cabinets) design, into finishes and materials, and into the kinds of pieces that are offered and from which one must select—desk or secretary, armoire or dresser, seating module, or love seat.

Upholstered Furniture

The family of upholstered furniture includes almost any kind of seating piece that has been upholstered—fabric covering inner construction and filling. This can range from the longest sofa or complement of seating units to a tiny boudoir chair. The quality of an upholstered piece derives from frame construction, filling, fabric, tailoring, and frame finish, should part of the frame be exposed. Because so much is hidden from the eye, upholstery shopping can be a "blind" experience unless one knows what to look for. Fortunately, manufacturers are required by law to label all materials used in upholstery, and at a reliable store an informed salesperson can help to translate this information and to give you an accurate "reading."

Usually the better-grade filling and cover, the more handwork that goes into the frame construction, webbing and springs, and finish and tailoring, the higher the cost and the better the quality. Nevertheless, the price is no real guarantee, and what you are searching for is the best value, not the biggest price. So shop at a store that will stand behind its products, that has a reputation for honesty.

There are certain basics to look for, yourself, that will give you a quick indication of how well a piece is made. By feeling the sofa or chair all over, you can tell whether or not there are any holes or any hollow areas, whether or not the frame is close to the surface and might eventually push through. Note the quality of the seaming and the number of seams—which will tell you how much piecing has been done. Check to see that the design is as well upholstered on the sides and back as on the front and if the fabric pattern has been properly positioned on frame and on cushions.

Trying out the sofa by sitting on it will tell you something immediately about its comfort, resiliency, arm height, and cushion softness. Your needs here will be based on personal preference.

The Fabric Must Also Be Right

If you have a certain texture or pattern in mind, be sure to check this out with your salesman; it may not work on a sofa with lots of tufting or be right for the kind of climate where you will use it. Hidden selling points, such as how well the frame is joined, seat construction, back construction, pillow and cushion filling, will have to be uncovered by your salesperson, based on his personal acquaintance with the product and the manufacturer.

As you begin to get an overview of what is available in upholstered furniture, you will automatically get the feel of what to look for, using the guidelines described above. You will also be much more familiar with what is actually available, what the price ranges and brackets are for each style, what store or stores carry the better-made and/or better-priced product.

You will have seen all kinds of sofas, from small love seats with exposed frames to totally upholstered, modern seven-footers. You will have observed all the variations in the styling of contemporary modular seating designs as well as all the possible skirt treatments for the more traditional sofa and chair designs.

There is an enormous range of lounge or club and the lighter "pull-up" chair on the market, so your window shopping should include a perusal of every kind of chair now manufactured.

Wood Furniture

While you are window shopping for upholstered furniture, you will also be checking out table and cabinet designs, not only to see what is available in your style mood, but what kinds of individual pieces are manufactured in this design genre.

There are quality checkpoints in the buying of case pieces, but most of these points are visible, not hidden, as with upholstery. Sturdiness of construction, quality of veneers, finish and hardware can be evaluated by the observer simply by a careful inspection of any given piece. Again, it helps to have an informed salesperson point out the advantages and fine points of any design you are considering.

Because wood has been and still is the primary material used for case furniture, the manufacture of such furniture has always been handled in relation to the propensity of wood to dry out or attract moisture, to swell or shrink. Continual improvements in the veneering process over the centuries has ensured the production of wood furniture that will stay glued and will not tend to peel or crack easily: It is not essential to know all the technical expertise that goes into manufacturing today that makes such potential problems almost nonexistent in veneered furniture. Of course a certain amount of furniture is made of solid wood, which has its advantages, such as ease of carving and refinishing, not to mention the fact that there is no veneered surface that can be pierced or chipped off. Current manufacturing techniques also allow for possible expansion and shrinking of wood to ensure the stability of the finished solid-wood design as well.

Finish

The finishing of wood furniture will not only enhance its beauty but also underscore its formal or country mood, its decorative impact. Unless you expect to open a finishing plant, it is hardly necessary for you to absorb a textbook rundown of finishing procedures. Suffice it to say that wood furniture goes through many finishing processes, from initial sanding and bleaching to staining, shading, distressing, glazing, lacquering, and rubbing. Some furniture designs, such as the country style, handcraft-looking pieces, are given a much more simplified finishing than elegant, formal styles with highly enameled surfaces. Again, it is the style of the furniture design and the suitability of the finish rather than its complexity that determines whether a piece of furniture is right for your room.

With the aid of an informed salesman and your own good vision, you can quickly appraise the merits of any wood furniture piece, checking out uniformity of veneering and finishing, smoothness of all surfaces, including the inside of doors and drawers, the good fit and use of dovetailing in drawers, matched veneering in table leaves, well-scaled, attractively finished, and securely attached pulls and hinges. Make sure the design has stability, is not top-heavy or made with spindly, wobbly legs.

Furniture woods fall into two basic categories—softwoods, such as pine, which come from evergreens, and hardwoods, such as maple, which derive from trees with broad, flat leaves. It is the graining of the wood rather than its "hard" or "soft" category that usually decides whether it is to be used for formal or country-style furniture. Maple and pine, for instance, are both favored for the more informal, casual furniture designs. Most popular furniture woods are as follows:

Maple: A strong, hardy wood with a yellowish-red cast used for Colonial designs and other informal furniture styles.

Walnut: Durable with a fine luster; graining varies from plain to decorative. Stability makes it a popular cabinet wood.

Mahogany: Dark wood with reddish tones, offering a wide choice of grain figuration. Takes a high polish and is warp-resistant.

Oak: A hardy, coarsely grained wood favored for Jacobean furniture and used today for casual-style reproductions as well as contemporary designs.

Pine: Another strong, durable wood, usually given a dark finish similar to oak and having a luster. New light or "stripped" pine country pieces have dull or matte finishes and pale yellow tone, are popular choices for country-style rooms.

Cherry: The most popular of the fruitwoods, favored for formal eighteenth-century English and American design. Usually given a rich brown finish. Other fruitwoods are pear and apple.

Birch: A pale wood that can be stained or enameled with ease and has handsome graining in its yellow variation. Strong and hard-wearing.

Teak: A wood often used for contemporary cabinet design, comes in a range of tones and often with figured graining.

Rosewood: A favored choice for eighteenth-century French and English designs, today it is utilized for elegant modern cabinetry. A dark wood that can be highly polished.

Others: Satinwood, hickory, pecan, chestnut, tulipwood, ebony, ash, and yew are among other woods less frequently used but offering still further variation in wood graining and color potential.

Mixing and Matching of Furniture Woods and Finishes

You may already have discovered, for yourself, a basic contradiction in the way professional designers work with wood finishes and the way they are displayed and sold in department and furniture stores. Interior designers prefer to mix woods and finishes rather than match them, because they know that this is a sure way of making a room more personal and interesting. A store, on the other hand, wants to display an entire collection within the same area, so that the customer can immediately see all that is available in a specific furniture grouping.

The more innovative stores are moving away from this kind of merchandising, encouraging and encouraged by today's greater emphasis on a freer, more individual approach to interior design. Of course this mixing of styles and finishes is not a new concept. Just take a look at rooms from historic restorations and you will discover that our ancestors mixed more than they matched. That's because no one ever went out to a furniture store and bought everything in one fell swoop. Furniture was handed down from generation to generation, with new pieces added whenever they could be afforded.

Safer to Mix

There's a safety factor that also encourages the use of mixed rather than matched finishes. If additional pieces are needed—at some future time when one moves into a larger home with more spacious rooms—it is often impossible to find the same style and finish, especially if the collection is no longer being manufactured. Using a mixture right from the start ensures a built-in flexibility that makes it much easier to add new pieces to current possessions.

Mixing painted and stained finishes has always been a treatment in period rooms, and also allows for greater flexibility than the matched-finish look. Today's modern counterpart to these painted finishes is the high-gloss enamel favored for sleek-lined Parsons-style tables and other hard-edged cabinetry.

Mixing wood furniture with metal, plastic, and such outdoor materials as rattan and wicker is still another way of achieving textural and color diversity and a more personal style. Tables and étagères of chrome, brass, or steel with glass, or curved chairs molded from opaque plastics and plexiglass, are frequent companions to furniture fashioned from conventional woods. So are chairs, chaises, tables, cabinets, and even bed frames crafted from wicker, rattan, cane, bamboo, and other tropical materials.

In addition to offering a charming change of pace, furniture made from materials other than wood also present lower-priced alternatives. One can improvise with a pair of wicker chairs in that first living room, for example, eventually moving those chairs into a family room or den in the next home, if so desired.

At the other end of the price spectrum are antiques, which today are so costly that only the rich or the lucky can afford more than one or two. Of course authentic antiques offer the character of age and patina in a way that no reproduction can emulate. On the other hand, many reproductions are rescaled to fit today's smaller rooms, and have the great durability afforded by modern manufacturing technology.

Balance Upholstery with Cabinetry

In planning the furniture arrangement, you will discover a need to use cabinets to balance off areas of upholstery, to position tables and desks to "hold down" the decor, to give it character and definition. The style of the furniture also relates to the proportion of upholstery to case pieces. So does the basic decorating approach. In doing your homework, you may have noticed that authentic interiors of eighteenth-century France, England, or America used more tables and cabinets. Modern settings tend to emphasize seating, especially when space is at a premium. Contemporary floor lamps or built-in lighting often serve the same purpose as lamps on end tables, and obviously take up much less room.

Functional Furniture

The specific furniture pieces that you choose for each room of your house will be determined by the function of that room to a large extent. But as you go along you will see that there is often more than one way to answer a need, fulfill a requirement; sometimes there are several possible alternatives.

You will be dealing with this more concretely as you nail down the floor plan, a subject with which we deal in the next section. But at the furniture canvassing stage of your decorating project, you should be aware of the fact that these alternatives exist and begin to explore the possibilities.

Clothing in the bedroom can be stored in a dresser, a chest, a chest-on-chest, a highboy, or an armoire. Nightstands can flank a bed, but a writing table or small cabinet could easily substitute for one of the night tables.

Is your living room to have a secondary seating arrangement or would you prefer to install some kind of study area with a desk and chair? Self-contained furniture groupings may free wall space for a tall cabinet or secretary, which will supply balance as well as storage. Or would you prefer to use a standing card-table arrangement that can also be utilized for informal dining?

It's time now to go back to those magazines from which you cut photographs of rooms that contained color schemes or decorating ideas. Look once again at those rooms still in these books (as well as those that were clipped); you may spot some interesting and unexpected furniture choices. Get used to looking at what is in a room—on your trips to model rooms or decorator showrooms. You'll see that talented designers are not only creative with color, pattern, and style but they can also be innovative in the way they arrange furniture and the kind of pieces they choose.

You may prefer to follow the more conventional route and choose a conservative approach. On the other hand, just knowing that such alternatives exist and can be most attractive and interesting may loosen you up, may help you develop some flair. Breaking out of the conventional mold, doing something a little different, a bit unexpected, will give your rooms the warm personal touch that's so desirable.

Furniture Arrangement

Furniture arrangement is a blueprint, a strategy that maps out what furniture pieces are to go into a room and where they will be placed. It is the final solution to the puzzle—the puzzle of space.

All of us have admired rooms that possessed a wonderfully cohesive quality, a marvelous balance of scale and proportion, a pleasing and interesting juxtaposition of furniture. We have also been in rooms that seem too empty or too cluttered, with little sense of spatial flow or continuity. Often these rooms are lopsided—too much furniture on one side of the room—or cavernous—with all the pieces pushed against the walls.

The harmonious interiors that we find so pleasing could never have been created without an inspired floor plan to serve as a guide. Their "natural" grace results from hours of experimental, trial-and-error planning until the final arrangement ultimately emerges. Jumbled rooms are exactly what they seem to be—thrown together with little, if any, advance preparation and design.

Make a Floor Plan on Paper

By experimental planning, we're not suggesting a moving back and forth of heavy sofas or cabinets. Let your fingers do the pushing by creating a floor plan on paper. All you need is graph paper, pencils, erasers, scissors, ruler, tracing paper, and cardboard. And you must know the exact dimensions of your room and the measurements of any openings—doors, windows, fireplaces, alcoves. These specifications are the spatial limits within which you must work. The room's major purpose or living role establishes the requirements you must fulfill.

Naturally, you will approach the design of a living-room floor plan one way, a bedroom arrangement another way. The reasons are obvious—the basics, or primary pieces, to be used for these rooms represent different priorities—living and entertaining as opposed to sleeping and storage. While we will discuss the arrangement problems relevant to each and every kind of room in Part III of this book, we feel that it is useful at this stage of decorating to outline the basic principles and procedures used in developing a room arrangement or floor plan.

Whether you are designing a room completely from scratch or moving to a new home (and planning to keep most of your furniture), creating a floor plan is a great hedge against serious error. You will avoid the trap of buying furniture first and then trying to arrange it later, and you will know in advance just how your present pieces will fit into the new home. This will facilitate moving and help you eliminate "hopeless" pieces if you have any—rather than trying to take them with you.

For your floor plan you will need one-fourth-inch graph paper, letting each quarter-inch marking represent a linear foot, each box a square foot. Carefully measure floor, walls, openings, and all protrusions—jogs, beams, air conditioners, radiators—with a ruler and mark accordingly on the graph. Then make cutouts or templates from cardboard of each piece of furniture you expect to use applying the same one-fourth-inch-to-a-foot ratio.

Assess the architecture of the room. Does it have a natural focal point, such as a fireplace, or does the furniture arrangement have to serve this purpose in addition to other functions? Are attractive elements to be dramatized, such as a bay window or paneled wall, or must the furniture compensate for boxy, sterile architecture?

Check out the natural traffic patterns. If the room is a pass-through from one area to another, this major traffic lane must be kept open. If the room has only one entrance, then the traffic lanes will be those avenues by which one approaches the major and secondary furniture groupings. Mark off the traffic lanes with one of your colored pencils; notice that they will divide the room into major and minor areas.

In plotting your scheme, avoid putting all the heavy pieces on one side of the room and grouping lightly scaled designs on the other. Try to achieve balance wherever you can. A large cabinet in a dark finish, for example, will balance a bulky cluster of upholstered designs on the other side of the interior.

Choose furniture whose scale is in proportion to the room, avoiding massive pieces for tiny rooms or delicate designs for spacious interiors.

Vary shapes, counterpointing curves with straight lines. Avoid the repetition of shapes—such as using large rectangular coffee tables in two different furniture groupings in the same room. Make one table round or oval or use a pair of small tables.

Strive for a balance in heights, but don't put too much variation within a room. Too many eye levels can be jarring, can detract from the overall harmony of the arrangement.

Don't cluster pattern in one area; spread it around rather than concentrating it on one major piece. Pulling it into other areas via pillows, draperies, a skirted table, etc., will also help the balance.

Integrate your conversation groups but let the individual pieces "breathe," have some air around them. No furniture should ever touch the wall; there should be some space between the wall and sofa.

Try to play around with arrangements that avoid the perimeter look —furniture placed only around the walls. Position near the walls those pieces that cannot be free-standing—that are not finished on four sides, such as a cabinet, dresser, or storage modules. Most furniture is finished on all sides—upholstered designs, desks, tables.

Start your plan with the absolute musts—the pieces that have top priority—and then build your scheme around them.

Avoid empty holes, but do not overfill the space. Aim for an effect somewhere in between. Don't jam furniture together even if you prefer a somewhat cluttered look. The style of your decor will also dictate the degree of clutter. The contemporary "minimal" school of decorating favors the sleek look of built-ins and banquettes and a low-key use of accessories. Country living, on the other hand, emphasizes the cozy hospitality of plentiful furniture and a rich cornucopia of bucolic accents and accessories.

Don't look only to furniture for balance in height and scale. Tall screens, large paintings, oversized mirrors, and ornamental window treatments also contribute to the overall composition.

Try out many possible arrangements. To do this make templates of several different sofa lengths and various cabinet sizes. Copy each arrangement on tracing paper so you do not have to continually mark up new graph paper with the room dimensions.

Above all, be flexible. If the plan you hoped would work is not appropriate, look for the kind of alternatives we discussed earlier. Often a second choice proves to be more interesting than the first.

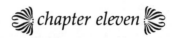
chapter eleven

Storage

Real estate agents jest that their clients look at the closets before they see the living room. But their joke is not far from the truth. In an effort to cut costs, builders of new homes and high-rises curtail the number of closets; indeed some of the so-called rooms in these new layouts are no bigger than the walk-in closets commonly found in pre-war houses and apartments.

So storage space is of paramount concern. With our television sets, stereo and movie equipment, home office files, hobby paraphernalia, assorted collectibles, and extensive wardrobes, we own many more possessions than our grandparents but have much less space in which to store them.

The answer to our problem is to create additional storage space within our homes. This is done with storage furniture that climbs the walls rather than eats up valuable floor space and with built-ins—the design of brand-new walls added onto the room and providing architectural enrichment as well as a wealth of storage area.

No home can run smoothly, nor can life be really comfortable, without adequate storage. Even if you're not a Felix character from "The Odd Couple" who is obsessed with neatness and order, it can be extremely frustrating to live in a disorderly home that results from lack of storage. The house is constantly cluttered with things that belong out of sight, and one is always on a treasure hunt, searching for one misplaced possession or another.

And so the most beautifully designed interior will soon be hidden under a morass of litter if proper storage has not been provided. Therefore, don't put your storage needs in escrow; make the necessary provisions an integral part of your floor plan. To do this you must evaluate your storage needs realistically and compute the storage potential of each and every room. By subtracting what you have from what you need, you will arrive at some general estimate (usually too low) of what must be provided. Then comes the next step: How will this be done?

Before you decide whether to use free-standing, built-in storage, or a combination of the two, you should review the kind of furniture tentatively scheduled to be purchased. Study each piece and see if some kind of substitution can be made. A console table in your foyer might now become a cabinet with drawers. Nightstands that are small cabinets offer more storage than simple tables; bookcase headboards are certainly more storage oriented than a four-poster. Perhaps a trundle bed, which has concealed storage space for linens, might be just the style for your son's bedroom. A decorative trunk could occupy the spot originally slated for a coffee table.

These are the kinds of changes you can make without altering the basic floor plan or character of the room. You are simply replacing single-purpose designs with pieces that are storage "worthy."

These replacements will not solve all your storage needs, but they should help. If the overflow is still significant, you will probably have to include some kind of storage wall—either built-in or free-standing.

Storage Furniture and Systems

We are very fortunate that so many furniture manufacturers now cater to the storage crisis. Their contributions are so extensive that an entirely new family or category of furniture design has emerged in the last generation: modular wall systems.

Modular storage systems contain individual upper and lower cabinet units that can be selected in a "building block" approach that will enable you to custom design your own storage wall. Upper units offer open shelf area for books, plants, accessories as well as dust-free space concealed behind cabinet doors—to house glass, television, and miscellany. Lower cabinets are fitted to store stereo equipment, tapes, records, bar paraphernalia, serving pieces, and other assorted possessions.

Writing tables, which sometimes extend for dining, or completely organized desk modules, or units specifically designed as sewing centers are often included as part of the total modular system.

These are available in just about every style and finish and in a broad spectrum of quality and price. There are elaborately compartmented and fitted modern designs offered in beautifully colored enamel finishes; there are collections that borrow design inspiration from Shaker and Colonial styles. Some manufacturers have now extended the modular concept for the new "great room" approach—in which upholstered furniture, wall units, and occasional tables are totally coordinated for the makings of an entire room.

The beauty of these wall systems is that one may use as much or as little as one needs and can afford. Budget limitations may suggest that you purchase a collection that is well established and will be around for a few years so that you can add as you can afford to. Or if you move there is a good chance that you will have more room for additional units as well as a greater need for them.

You can take free-standing units with you, arrange and rearrange them at will, move them from one room to another. The rather informal modular wall system that sheathed one wall of your first apartment living room may find a new home in a family room or possibly a child's room in the new house.

Modular storage units can frame a window or turn a corner; they can give you the look of custom-designed built-ins at a fraction of the cost. And there's an unexpected dividend: Wall systems contribute to the background enrichment of a room, often lending character to boxy, sterile architecture.

Another kind of wall system, though not as multifaceted or versatile, is the book-stack unit; they can be used singly, in pairs, or even in multiples for a completely covered wall. These kinds of wall units do not offer the almost unlimited type of storage potential available with the many diverse units of a modular system, but they usually offer some variation in upper and lower cabinet design. These are wonderful choices for dens and libraries, as alternates for the built-in bookcase wall. Used in multiples, they can substitute for a china cabinet or hutch in a dining room or area, providing enormously expanded storage potential.

Armoires, which are made in streamlined contemporary interpretations as well as in traditional designs, offer greater storage space than the usual cabinet or dresser. And the armoire can be put anywhere in the house—bedroom, living room, dining room, even entrance foyer if space permits. If you happen to be the proud possessor of an antique armoire, you can have a cabinetmaker custom partition the inside to solve your specific storage requirements.

Built-ins

Of course nothing utilizes space any better than custom-designed built-in storage. This doesn't have to be more costly if it's done with inexpensive lumber or as a home project, but it is usually a permanent part of the house and cannot travel with you when you move.

A built-in bookcase wall that matches the paneling in a library is a beautiful as well as a wonderfully functional addition to your home, but this represents a sizable investment and should be contemplated only if you plan to stay.

Building in, to your own design, allows you to take whatever wall space is available and transform it into a super-storage wall. This can be done anywhere in the house—to create a wardrobe wall in the bedroom or dressing room, a serving and storage wall in the dining room, complete with its own built-in lighting, custom storage for a hobby center, or a home office, and even double-depth cabinets that provide additional storage concealed behind the surface layer, which swings out in sections to reveal what is behind.

Custom storage can convert any wall of your home into a storage haven, sometimes by eating up only a foot of floor space. It can also maximize the use of dead space in recesses and alcoves, under window ledges, under a stairwell, in a back hallway, in and around the plumbing in a bathroom. Refitting an existing closet with well-engineered built-ins can maximize the closet's storage potential.

Today, built-in as well as free-standing storage units are often designed with adjustable shelves, supported by wood dowels that fit into holes drilled vertically down the length of the cabinet, so that you can create your own kind of inner division. Taking this one step further are the assorted storage systems that utilize standards and brackets, offering the flexibility of free-standing design and the look of a built-in wall. Metal-framed storage systems also provide flexible, ready-made storage. Designed originally for commercial use, they are usually less costly.

Naturally, it is much more expensive and more complicated to build in storage walls that have cabinet drawers and doors. One way to get around this, especially for the home-done project, is to build in open shelving and then install regular window shades (which can be laminated or embellished) at the top of each section. These can pull all the way down to cover the shelves and to add protection from dust at the same time.

Built-in storage can be designed with its own recess for a small sofa or convertible love seat. The simplest kind of storage wall—often chosen for kitchens or basements—is one of pegboard from which can be suspended shelves and individual items.

Sometimes an entire room can be built in—a combination of banquettes and wall storage, or a bed and storage for clothing. This approach is especially popular in vacation homes where rooms are small and often have to play a multipurpose role.

Certain architectural deficits as well as space shortages may influence your choice of custom built-ins for one room and free-standing units for another. Protruding jogs and air conditioners, awkward alcoves, an unwanted window, ugly pipes and radiators can all be camouflaged by inventive built-in cabinetry. Built-ins are sometimes the only choice when a bedroom comes with no closet of its own. Professionals will build in ceiling-high armoires on one wall and place the bed in the recess between, thereby creating excellent storage space and architectural character at the same time.

It really pays to call in an expert when installing a built-in storage system. A skilled technician may be more expensive, but he will give you the durability, fit, and quality finishing that you would want from free-standing furniture.

If you are very handy, however, and would like to do some of the less challenging projects yourself—at least at the start—there are numerous books on the market that will take you through every phase of building it yourself, complete with excellent step-by-step diagrams. Beginning with closets and possibly some projects for the basement or family room, you might become facile enough to eventually tackle very extensive built-in cabinetry for the most important rooms of your house.

An effort should be made to tie the surface color of the built-in wall into the decor of the room. Wood finish should match any paneling in the room, otherwise the unit should be given the same paint color as the wall or repeat the color used for flooring, or at least one major piece in the room. If treated independently, it will look like a design

POWER-TRAC RESIDENTIAL TRACK LIGHTING BY HALO

UPHOLSTERY FABRICS OF HERCULON

INTERIOR DESIGN AND FURNISHINGS BY W&J SLOANE.

(Top Left) A dark apartment alcove becomes an animated dining area, thanks to the track lighting stretched above, and a fascinating mélange of furniture, which includes the modern pedestal table, cane, wood and chrome chairs, and antique serving cabinet. Ornately framed family portraits contrast with the simple and contemporary tabletop elements.

(Top Right) A freewheeling mix of colors, patterns, and furniture, in some very unexpected combinations, are surprisingly pleasing in this lively living room. Wall coverings abound; there's even one on the ceiling. Note too the variety of colors chosen for the fabrics, these lifted from the tones of the geometric-design dhurrie rug. Room designed by Thayer Coggin.

(Bottom) Dining right in the living room can be as formal as you please. And, as you can see, this living-dining interior by W & J Sloane is enriched by elegant furniture designs, opulent fabrics, and luxurious appointments. Louis XVI chairs surround oval dining table. Draperies, tied back high, dramatize tall windows.

A sense of humor can create a visual
delight. Bearing witness to this fact is
this black-and-white modern kitchen,
amusingly punctuated by the startling
red of an oversized exhaust hood. Cabinet surfaces, counter tops, and backsplashes are all of glowing, white
Formica. Notice, also, the interesting
sculpture-like shape of the butcher-
block-topped work island.

ft) Once the all-white kitchen evoked spital-like sterility; today it can be the st dramatic room of the house. What ds this stark-white kitchen its unde- ble excitement is a vibrant floral stripe ll covering, colorful serving pieces and essories, a bevy of hanging plants and ted trees. Dining island doubles as a rk and menu-planning center.

(Right) Typical, galley-shaped apartment kitchen gets an unusual design treatment. Upper cabinets are sheathed with giant blowups of vegetable-theme photographs custom printed by a professional color lab. A protective coat of polyurethane, added once the blowups have been applied, ensures ease of cleaning and durability.

(Top) *A few delicious touches of citrus hues add interest and vitality to a bedroom in a tropical retreat framed almost completely in the cooling expanses of stark white. Even the flooring of vinyl tile is as white as the fabrics. Trim and tailored roman shades permit a view of the ocean.*

(Bottom) *Crisp greens of leafy fabric and wallpaper print, and breezy wicker furniture, lighten a room that plays on the one-pattern look, accented by hot-house colors in the pillows and the modern canvas. Protruding jog at far end of the room becomes a niche for built-in banquette. Designed by Edmund Motyka.*

"stepchild" and fail to provide the sleek, streamlined look that built-ins usually supply.

Whether installing free-standing or custom built-in storage, decide in advance just how much open (bookshelves) and how much concealed storage you really need. The proper allotment will depend upon the kind and amount of possessions to be stored. Certain belongings should be hidden in drawers or behind cabinet doors, but other items, such as beautiful sculpture, porcelains, and of course plants, should be displayed so they can be seen. A mix of open shelves with cabinets is usually more interesting than a completely covered storage wall, although in a bedroom the latter is often more desirable. How free your home remains from dirt and grit should also influence the kind of storage you would favor.

A popular solution to the storage dilemma, one favored by some professionals, is a built-in environment of laminated shelves, banquettes, cabinets, desks, platform beds, and so on. This approach uses a matte-finished plastic laminate to construct such an environment; the laminate is often the same color as the walls. These built-in architectural solutions make extremely efficient use of limited space or of small rooms. Sleek and streamlined, they create a flow of space even in cramped quarters. But they are custom designed and installed for a specific room; they will never work nearly as well anywhere else. So consider how long you expect to stay before you make an investment in something that you will probably have to leave behind.

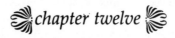

chapter twelve

Space Expanders

With space at a premium, today's smaller rooms often have to serve a larger role. An entrance hall is suddenly the scene for dining, a studio living room becomes a bedroom, part-time children's rooms serve as dens most of the year. What makes it happen, what gives these rooms their two-sided character, is furniture that is dual purpose by design or else manipulated to serve a secondary role.

Convertibles

The best known and most often used of all dual-purpose furniture designs is the convertible sofa, although these days, dual sleep designs can also be love seats, chairs, or ottomans, or part of a modular seating group. As guest rooms have literally disappeared from the American scene and as the one-room studio apartment multiplies with every high-rise that is built, dual-sleep furniture is often the cornerstone around which an entire room is built.

The skyrocketing need for convertible seating has prompted not only a wider choice in styling, which runs the gamut from sleek contemporary to formal traditional, but has also led furniture producers to develop new manufacturing techniques. Bulky inner construction has been refined so that today many convertible sofas are virtually indistinguishable from a "twin" design that does not contain concealed pull-out bedding. No longer is one forced to purchase a clunky-looking sofa that quickly belies its other role; new convertibles are as sleek, versatile, and varied as any other sofa.

This is also true for chair designs that also recline, swivel, and rock. Gone is the overweight, cumbersome recliner; today we have many handsome designs that transform from a conventional chair into a comfortable design for reading, relaxing, even television viewing. These new streamlined designs allow you to buy one chair that does the work of two or three, hence cutting down on what you must spend and keeping the furnishing of a small room to a minimum.

In shopping for a sofa-bed, look for value rather than the low price tag. Check it out the same way you would a conventional sofa, but be sure also to examine the ease with which the open and close mechanism works. Also note sturdiness of construction; look for desirable rounded edges (so that sheets do not tear) and check the size and height of the opened bed.

While you will not have to accept less than a beautifully styled design in convertible seating, expect to pay more than you would for a comparable sofa—to cover manufacturer's added expense of the sleep mechanism. Less costly alternatives to convertibles are daybeds. Here back cushions are removed and the mattress cushion takes linens and blankets. The daybed, unlike the convertible, is a single bed, and has to be made up each time it is used. The convertible conceals linens as well as bedding.

Dual-purpose Designs

Other alternatives to hidden sleep facilities include trundle beds and contemporary versions of the old Murphy bed, now encased in its own cabinet rather than hidden in a closet. Double-decker bunk beds of course are space savers, as they offer sleeping for two but take up only the floor space of a single bed.

Dual-purpose tables are a part of our own decorative heritage—the rustic chair-table was a charming concept in Colonial times (the rounded back of a tall wooden chair flops down to become a tabletop). Gateleg leaf tables were also popular for small Early American rooms; and contemporary drop-leaf versions serve admirably today in apartments and houses of limited space.

The drop-leaf table is just one form of the expandable table; consoles that pull open to take leaves and flip-top tables, whose folded top is slid aside and then opened, are other very popular versions. These are extremely useful in apartments that have no dining room, as they can be positioned in a foyer, or placed against a wall or behind the sofa in the living room, occupying a minimum of space when not extended for dining.

And there are still other types of "now you see it, now you don't" table strategies. These include coffee tables that spring up to dining height, extension tables that most of the time stand as shallow consoles within a wall system, tables that are totally enclosed within a cabinet of a storage wall, and benches and ottomans that conceal a practical table surface of plastic laminate beneath the comfortable top cushions.

Tables That Nest or Bunch

The nest of tables, in which three or four tables of identical style but different size nest or store within each other, has long been a cherished space saver. Today they are often expressed in sleek modern designs and in new materials; those of molded plastic are extremely light in weight and even easier to use. New manufacturing techniques and modern plastics have also given birth to the nest of chairs—or stackables—chairs that stack on one another in a trim and attractive manner so that they can be kept out in full view rather than crowding a closet.

Bunching tables—tables that group together to form one large rectangle or even a circle but can be used singly—offer still another opportunity to stretch space and double the utility of a single design. Often these bunching tables are on casters, so they can easily be moved over to another chair or furniture grouping at a far end of the room.

Designers of these table space savers are guided by two principles: (1) that one piece does the work of two and (2) that several pieces occupy the space of only one. Today's apartment dweller owes a great deal to the imagination and ingenuity of these talented furniture designers.

Dual-purpose and nesting furniture represent one way to save on space. Another is to more fully maximize existing space by the way you utilize or position your furniture.

.Maximizing Space

Grouping furniture into conversation pits, using a free-standing bed (a full bed or one with a headboard finished on four sides), and arranging furniture on an angle rather than parallel or perpendicular to the walls frees wall space for additional storage furniture and of course, also contributes a fresh, innovative look.

And if you look around you, at your rooms, at the way they are presently arranged, you may discover all kinds of unexploited possibilities that can multiply the space you own. Two much-needed benches or ottomans can slide under a writing table, a console table, or a sofa table. Placing an étagère (perhaps slim-lined metal and glass designs) on either side of the sofa on a long wall will give your room an effective focal point, extra storage, and yet take up a minimum of floor space.

Étagères are also extremely versatile space dividers, establishing a sense of separation between the dining and living areas of a one-room apartment without really cutting off the flow of space. They're wonderful storage designs, especially for collectibles and plants; if used as a divider, the lower shelves can double as a serving surface for the dining area.

Putting covered baskets wherever and whenever feasible is still another marvelous and yet inexpensive way of stretching space. Rectangular baskets can store under square coffee tables; the really big sizes substitute beautifully for coffee or end tables, doubling, if they are brass, as storage bins.

You can store baskets in full sight on top of the soffits in your kitchen, on the lower shelf of a Welsh cupboard, on the top shelf of wall systems, in the empty space beneath a console table, or at the foot of a bed.

Make a space-shy study area work efficiently by constructing a desk from two low file cabinets (these come in wonderful colors now) and a top of wood or plastic laminate.

Discover hidden seating potential. A long low windowsill, or a shelf created by a low wall of built-ins, converts into a spot to sit upon simply by the addition of the necessary cushions.

Don't overlook the double-duty potential of chests and trunks. Old ones add great character to a room; new ones can be extremely elegant and decorative. These can also be used as coffee or occasional tables, at the foot of a bed, in an entrance hall, or perhaps even under a tall console table.

The peripatetic tea cart that rolls from dining room to kitchen to bedroom is the kind of nomadic furniture that stretches space in a small home and is a great convenience in a large one. It is simply used wherever needed at the moment, and is especially wonderful at clean-up time, since all the dirty dishes inevitably get rolled into the kitchen in a single trip.

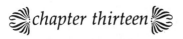

chapter thirteen

Lighting

Anyone who has ever been to the theater has come to appreciate the lighting technician's craft, the wizardry that transforms the warm and cozy living-room set into an eerie backdrop for murder or intrigue or changes an ordinary street scene into a setting for romance. Yet how often do we exploit lighting as a tool—to envoke mood and drama—or even to enhance decoration?

The anonymous and often repetitive room shapes in apartments and houses constructed today encourage our seeking fresh and new ways to create a more personal environment. While we may have become more venturesome in our use of color and texture, in the way we mix designs and style moods, we still tend to utilize lighting merely as a necessary afterthought—as an accessory or to satisfy visual requirements but little more. In doing this, we overlook one of the most powerful, flexible, and fascinating decorating tools that modern technology has put at our disposal.

The ideal conditions for planning the best possible lighting for one's home are limited to those who can sit down with an architect and a lighting consultant at the time the home is in the blueprint stage—or even earlier. Here, all the lighting can be designed from scratch, all the possibilities explored. But for most of us, our lighting must deal with an existing shell, specific wiring limitations, as well as a nucleus of furniture and other possessions. Yet even within this narrow framework, there is much that we can do with lighting to enhance and improve our rooms.

The Roles of Lighting

First we must begin to appreciate the many roles that light can and should play in room design. We quickly see the need for a light on a nightstand or on a desk, for lamps on two end tables that flank a sofa. But these specific functional roles of lighting represent only one part of the total picture.

In the first place, lighting provides general illumination—enough light so that a room is usable at night as well as during the day. Lighting also provides for specific functions, such as for reading, study, kitchen work, and so on. Lighting dramatizes or highlights special features in a room—a brick fireplace, a textured wall, paintings, plants, reflective surfaces. And lighting creates mood—dramatic, bold, intimate, soft, serene, mysterious, warm, romantic.

Lighting serves as an emotional and psychological tonic; it can excite or sedate, it can wake up or tone down. With improper or inadequate lighting, even the most fascinating mélange of furnishings seems drab and lifeless. Conversely, imaginative lighting techniques can breathe personality and style into a low-cost, underfurnished room. Lighting can also enlarge space by making walls recede, or give a shimmering glow to colors in fabrics and paintings.

General Lighting

For a room to be effectively "decorated," not merely supplied with lighting, its illumination must be a skillful blend of general or diffused and specific or task lighting. When only general, soft lighting is provided, a room lacks sparkle and atmosphere. Task or accent lighting, projecting a stronger beam, not only highlights specific objects or features, but also creates a play of glow and shadow, which enhances the ambiance and mood of the interior.

For many years, general lighting was supplied by ceiling fixtures and chandeliers, but to provide adequate light such fixtures gave off an unpleasant glare. Today, chandeliers are used primarily for decorative accent or for specific lighting over dining tables. General illumination installed today usually takes the form of built-in, structural lighting or the versatile add-ons, such as protruding light panels or track lighting, which are usually less complicated to install.

Lighting that is built in or added on to ceilings or walls has certain obvious advantages. It can be custom designed for the specific room and the specific activities. It does not take up valuable floor space or table surface, as table and floor lamps do. More than that, it provides another kind of lighting for a room, one that works in conjunction with portable lighting.

Built-in lighting usually takes the form of downlights, which include pinpoint and reflector spotlights, hi-hats and wall washers, or is provided by recessed ceiling panels. These can not only establish general illumination but provide specific functional lighting, dramatize individual elements, and offer safety and comfort in such areas as entrance foyers, hallways, stairways, and steps. Partially hooded wall washers that swivel can bathe an area with light, calling attention to a natural texture or marvelous color in a painting. And you can vary the kind of bulb used in built-in downlights to provide a concentration of light or a general glow.

Downlights, Uplights, and Track Lighting

If it is not feasible to install built-in downlights, they can also be mounted on the surface of the ceiling, assuming that wiring is sufficient. Often natural recesses can be utilized to install fluorescent tubes, such as on the soffits or underneath the upper cabinets in a kitchen, behind a window cornice or valance, or simply on a wall that partially recedes. A built-in effect can also be achieved by boxing in a tube.

Uplights, small units that sit on the floor, also provide general as well as specific illumination and work of course in counterpoint with downlights to create some very interesting and dramatic effects.

For general and specific lighting in small or work areas, paneled ceiling lighting, either built-in or surface-mounted, is especially effective because the glass or plastic cover diffuses the light evenly and with a lovely glow.

Track lighting, first developed for display purposes in retail stores, was quickly adopted as an enormously flexible method of residential lighting. Track lighting can approximate the custom effects of built-in units in a much simpler, less costly installation. Moreover, designers of track systems have demonstrated great invention in their choice of materials and refinement of shapes for the individual lamp holders.

Recessed ceiling lights provide ample illumination for desk and storage areas in this small but compact home office. Designer Noel Jeffrey used mellow-toned and richly textured birch for this sleek contemporary work space. Note that the dropped ceiling allows enough room for the downlights to be installed.

HALO POWER-TRAC LIGHTING BY McGRAW-EDISON

Shedding some light on music and art is a handy wall track unit, with fixtures that can be adjusted to light the keyboard and the sheet music, as well as to highlight assorted works of art, in this music corner of a large living room.

Set in from the walls, track lighting can be installed in a rectangle that emulates the proportions of the room, can be U-shaped, L-shaped, a single line, or any other possible variation wanted or needed.

A word should also be said here about wall fixtures, which are often used to serve a specific need such as at either side of a dressing-room mirror or over nightstands instead of lamps. When the design of such units features an open rather than a closed top, the light goes upward and bounces off the ceiling as well as downward for direct illumination.

Chandeliers and Lamps

Chandeliers, as we have mentioned earlier, have changed roles in the lighting scheme from an almost purely functional fixture to one that is primarily decorative, although for dining areas its role is a combination of both. Choosing a chandelier, for an entry or dining area, is often a problem, as we have seen from the fact that most people tend to buy undersized designs that are too small for the area. To play it safe, choose one that is bigger than what you think you need and try it out in your room, if possible, before purchasing it.

A similar error is often made in the selection of lamps, but this error in choice of scale is usually compounded by additional mistakes involving height and design. Lamps should be placed around the room where they must supplement the work already being done by downlights and wall washers, uplights, panels, wall fixtures, and track lighting. They must not only supplement but also offer alternate ways of lighting a room to suit the various activities for which a room is used.

We seem to be saying here that one should provide as many lighting options as possible for a single room. Where a room is used for a multiplicity of purposes and at many times of the day—such as a living room or family room—such diversity is more than a luxury; it becomes a necessity. By providing a room with a comprehensive lighting system, one extends the refinement of light control, the very usefulness of the area. By putting ceiling units on dimmer switches, and by using three-way bulbs or multibulbed lamps with individual pulls, one can further multiply the lighting options for a single room.

Obviously, budget and wiring limitations may curtail one's lighting ambitions, but this is the ideal to be aimed for in any multi-use interior.

Getting back to lamps, let us add that there is a mistaken tendency to use too many lamp shapes, too many materials, and too many different lamp heights in the same room. One of the reasons that so many restoration interiors are so pleasing is that they were lit by candles; no ugly, bulbous, or awkward bases marred the symmetry and beauty of these rooms. We can take a leaf out of our ancestors' book and follow their example—keep lamp shapes similar and simple. Avoid the trendy; it might just be the grotesque. Stick with classic shapes, such as candlestick, urn, vase, temple jar, and other similar bases, gearing the material chosen (porcelain or brass, as opposed to wood or ceramic) and the degree of formality or informality expressed to the mood of the room.

To avoid a disparity in heights, lamps should be selected so as to compensate for differences in table heights. Shorter lamps go on taller tables, taller ones on shorter tables, thus maintaining a relative similarity of lamp level throughout the room. Again, this is done to make the lamps blend in with the room's design rather than to noticeably protrude.

If you are buying only contemporary lamp designs for your interior, you will find some very handsome shapes in solid geometrics as well as some forms that rival modern sculpture. Modern floor lamps are especially sleek and streamlined, replacing the clumsy, uninspired, and often downright unattractive designs of a generation ago. These days, professional designers love to use slim-lined versions of the ubiquitous "pharmacy" lamp, which pops up in as many traditional and eclectic interiors as modern settings. Fashioned with a movable hood and dimmer control, it provides refinement of specific lighting and salvages space once occupied by end table and lamp. We see these wonderfully versatile and understated designs wherever a spot of light is needed—at either side of a sofa or bed, in a reading corner, next to a writing table. Shorter versions of these pharmacy lamps are often used in the place of traditional table lamp designs.

Developing a Plan

How and where to proceed with a blueprint for lighting depends on a number of variables—existing wiring, uses of the room, decorative requirements, and budget. Any necessary rewiring, cost of installation and professional fees (for architect or lighting consultant) must be figured into the budget. If you are contemplating a major overhauling of your room's lighting system, it pays in the long run to use an expert electrician and the guidance of a qualified lighting specialist. You may be fortunate enough to be working with an interior designer with extensive lighting expertise; in point of fact, you should not choose a designer who does not understand lighting because he or she will be limited not only in terms of a lighting plan but in providing you with a realistic approach to color for all times of the day.

A room that is used and enjoyed in a variety of ways should be given a more complicated and sophisticated lighting system than an interior that plays a single role. Therefore, the lighting of a living room will be more complex and include a greater range of units than that of a bathroom or foyer. The amount of general illumination and specific or functional lighting you will need for each room will be determined by the kind and size of the room and the many or few ways you expect to use it.

You also have a choice in the kind of illumination you use—incandescent lighting, which imparts a warmer, richer glow, and fluorescent, a somewhat "colder" kind of lighting but more efficient in terms of energy used. New fluorescents have now been improved so that their light more closely resembles the incandescents. Both kinds of lighting can be used interchangeably in ceiling panels, strip or cornice lighting.

We seem to have an emotional tie to incandescent lighting, which most closely resembles the firelight that man has warmed himself by since the beginning of time. This kind of lighting enriches the warm colors of the wheel, but is not nearly as effective as fluorescents with the cooler tones, as it diminishes blues and violets. However, we may actually enjoy the color variation that this gives our rooms at sunset.

A good rule of thumb to follow in planning a lighting scheme is that more units of lower wattage, spread around the room, is usually more attractive and more effective than only a few fixtures using high-wattage bulbs or bulb combinations. Again this offers greater refinement of light control. And the interplay of opposing light forces, such as downlights and uplights, can create the kind of fascinating shadows that invest an interior with other kinds of patterns—with another dimension.

To lay out a general lighting plan for any room, you must first estimate what is needed for daylight use, even on the sunniest day. Then make an outline of those evening activities to take place in the room. These can vary; a living room, for example, can be the scene of a party, a place for intimate conversation, or even a quiet reading spot for one. If your living room plays this kind of multifaceted role, then your lighting strategy must account for a variety of needs.

INTERIOR DESIGN BY GEORG ANDERSEN FOR ELLEN LEHMAN MCCLUSKEY ASSOC., INC.

Sofa-length lighting strip not only brightens the seating area but also throws light upward to the ceiling in this dramatically modern living-room interior. The designer mixed velvet, leather, steel, and glass for a provocative play on texture.

Budget Considerations

Your budget limitations will allow you to install built-ins or rewire if necessary to install downlights, surface-mounted panels, or such simple, yet far less costly, installations such as cornices, brackets, valances, soffit or strip lighting, clamp-ons, clip-ons, socket lighting or picture lights.

Strip lighting, which is a favored device for makeup centers in the bathroom, can also be used elsewhere in the home for special effect. Today, you can buy strip lighting fixtures in a choice of sizes and finishes, running the gamut from sleek chrome bases to painted metal.

Clamp-ons are slim designs that can hook onto a shelf or simply sit on top of one, and are therefore especially effective for the mini-spot-lighting of *objets d'art* on a long storage wall. And they can even stand vertically to throw a small beam of light in any direction.

An idea borrowed from professional photographers is clip-on lights, those units that are used with versatility by these professionals to expertly light a set. Since their design is utilitarian rather than glamorous, choose them as an adventure in high-tech, as well as a very flexible and movable lighting aid that does not require expensive installation.

Socket lighting is still another way of creating interesting ceiling lighting that is added on rather than recessed. Some designers create jumbo ceiling fixtures simply by installing many such sockets in a rectangular arrangement.

Painting or picture lights, which can be attached above or below a picture, are still viable choices for illuminating wall art, and obviously much less costly than ceiling recessed spotlights, which can serve the same purpose.

Assessing your lighting needs, starting with any ceiling or wall installation, must be done in conjunction with a finished floor plan or furniture arrangement; otherwise you have no accurate way of judging where the light should go. You should use the tables in the plan as a base for the necessary portable lamps that will provide what is needed for concentrated or functional lighting. You may have to supplement these with floor lamps, possibly of the new, sleek, pharmacy style we described earlier.

Finally you will want to add lighting for accent or mood. If your ceiling installation is comprehensive enough, you will have the necessary wall washers and spotlights. But a similar effect can also be achieved with spotlights that sit on the floor or the often-used canister lights that are positioned on the floor with light directed upward.

How much you use of the available lighting within each room will be determined by the time of day, the specific activity, and the kind of mood that is desired.

New Lighting Concepts

Contemporary architects continue to search for new ways to give interiors as much natural light as possible, hence the popularity of such concepts as the window wall or the revival, in new forms, of the artist's skylight, which is also favored for updated traditional houses. The skylight concept can be emulated not only by built-in or surface-mounted ceiling panels but by the installation of stock skylights, offered in a range of sizes, shapes, and materials. This latter approach can totally change the look and function of an upstairs bedroom, a windowless kitchen, or a dingy dining room, especially when these areas are used more in daytime hours, such as in a vacation house.

For some time now, furniture manufacturers have been designing the larger genre of traditional cabinetry—armoires, china cabinets, bookcase units—with built-in lighting, which is decorative as well as functional. Modern additions to the light scene include the large family of illuminated tables—cubes and other solids of translucent plastic lit from within. From time to time, whole wall systems incorporating built-in lighting have been offered.

Professional designers love to play around with special effects. Light panels are installed in the spaces between beams in a country French room or protruding rafters radiate light from luminous undersides—plastic diffusers covering fluorescents set within each beam. The possibilities are endless, spurred on by today's interest and preoccupation with light as an art form; more and more of the new light "sculptures" appear in homes today as a fascinating accessory. Often, this new art form is expressed in terms of colored light rather than the conventional white lighting, and this too may eventually shape the way light is used within the home in the future.

But for today, at least, explore for yourself some of the many, often simple yet untried, ways that you can use light to play a much more effective and decorative role in your own home.

part three

THE ABCs OF ROOM DECORATION

Introduction

With portfolios filled to overflowing, you are now ready to put all the information and expertise you have absorbed to work for you. At this stage of the decorating game you will nail down color scheme, floor plan, and background treatment, as well as window dressing and rug design, for each and every room of your house. Most important, you will be selecting those furniture designs that will make these rooms work efficiently and comfortably in a style that matches your personal taste preferences and your way of life. As you go through this most important phase of interior design, you will see a specific look emerging. The look may be purist traditional or stark modern, a delightful country informality, a freewheeling mix, or a purposeful eclecticism. But it will be a look that gains an added dimension, the dimension that emerges out of the personal process of selection and rejection. It is a quality of taste, of individual style that makes your room unlike any other room, that says "This is my home" to entering friends and guests.

You will also discover that each room presents a separate challenge; there is no single formula that you can apply throughout your home, unless it is possibly one of color scheme and floor treatment. The specific challenge of each room will of course give focus to the decorating. A living room requires the establishment of a focal point; this problem takes care of itself in a bedroom (the bed) or a dining room (the dining table). Living-room decoration also offers more freedom of choice, since the prerequisites are not as rigid as that of a dining room or child's room. At the same time, traditionally single-purpose rooms such as bedrooms and dining rooms may now have to serve a variety of roles, and the decoration must accommodate this.

So with an overview of the entire home ever present, zero in on the decorating solutions for each of your rooms. There will be enough time, after you have finished each interior, to go back over it all and see if the individual decorating schemes hang together as a totality. Always be aware, when you are working on one room, what colors, floor treatments, and furniture styles have been used in any adjacent areas. This will help you maintain a necessary consistency and prevent you from having to make too many revisions later.

In aiming for this consistency, this pleasing flow from room to room, do not go overboard and create a completely matched effect. Each room is a special and unique living space, not just one cog in the "machine for living," no matter how popular this phrase has come to be.

Sometimes an exceptionally warm, comfortable, and decoratively pleasing home is simply an amalgam of favorite things—possessions collected slowly and lovingly over a period of time. But the marvelous effect is not as simple as it seems; what holds it together is the common denominator of superb taste, an intuitive sense of color, scale, and balance.

Our rooms do not always build from square one, or can be completed in a day. In many instances, we are starting with a small or substantial number of furnishings or we are designing from scratch but do not have the budget to finish the job. Whatever the circumstance, it still pays to have a blueprint, a plan to guide us, even if we make some changes or modifications as we go along. By establishing the basic "interior landscape" for each room of our home, we will be able to proceed as quickly or as slowly as necessary.

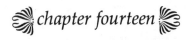

chapter fourteen

Living Rooms

The Victorian parlor, that overdecorated status symbol, roped off from the family and used only to receive and impress visitors, went into retirement long ago, as did antimacassars, horse-drawn carriages, and bustles. The American living room that has emerged since then has been prey to other fads and fancies, running the gamut from wildly baroque pattern-with-pattern indulgences to super-cool, perfectly engineered, space-age strategies.

Fortunately, today, the living room has emerged as a room in which all is possible and to which no one formula can or should apply. It can be richly romantic or embrace country-house comfort; it can have a convention-free spirit or a traditional discipline. But whatever the pervading style or mix of styles, living rooms today share a recurring theme—that of comfort, livability, and self-expression. The most important room of the house—sometimes the only room—the living room embodies and displays all those qualities and all those priorities that reflect and nourish the family that lives within it.

When a woman walks into a department store, views a wonderful model room and says, "I'll take it," she may have chosen the easiest route to interior design, but hardly the most intelligent—unless her living room is an exact duplicate of the architecture of the setting, and the designer who created it, her psychological and emotional twin. Decorating a room should be a slow and occasionally painful process; it's the way any creative effort works. But what comes out is a unique result, a synthesis of personal style and taste. There are no shortcuts that really succeed in the long run.

More Opportunity for Personal Expression

Living-room decoration offers the greatest potential for self-expression. For it is here that you can use the most extensive variety in kinds of furniture—sofas, chairs, ottomans, coffee tables, occasional tables, cabinets, secretaries, etc.,—and that you have greater freedom of choice in furniture arrangement. It is also the largest room of your home, the room on which the biggest chunk of the budget will be spent. It is a room that you will want to work beautifully for you and your family.

Living rooms also offer you a chance to play around with style, to mix and match, if that is your bag. The requisite number of cabinets in a bedroom or even a dining room may force the emergence of a fairly precise style, even though this can be softened by the choice of window dressing, bedspread, patterned or textured carpeting. But it takes a great deal of skill to blend, let us say, a dresser and chest of different finishes and style derivation.

In the living room a mixed effect is not only easier to evoke; it is also easier to control. A room of seating modules, for example, can balance or temper a wild combination of table designs. Conversely, a wonderful modern concept, such as a coffee table of glass on lucite or scroll-shaped lacquer, can instantly update traditional upholstery.

Unless you're a confirmed purist, chances are that your living room will reflect a fair amount of mixing, depending upon to what degree you need to express a specific look. If you tend toward country living but dislike anything too quaint, you might combine streamlined sofas with hand-hewn tables and cabinets. Perhaps you prefer modern interiors but have a weakness for period styles as well. A pair of bergères or Chinese Chippendale bamboo-framed chairs might be all that is needed to give your contemporary room just enough traditional flavor.

The photographs of favorite looks that you've put inside your living-room portfolio should tell you a great deal about the kind of style mood you like and the way professionals have achieved it. They should also indicate the degree of mixing that was done, and how it was achieved. Look closely at each piece of furniture; you may not have realized that there were so many modern tables or French chairs. Search beyond the overall impact to discover the individual elements that produced the wonderful chemistry.

Key Decor to Size and Style of Your Room

The architecture and the size of your room will set certain limitations. The mood of the furniture should bear some relationship to the style of the room, and the amount of space available will determine, more or less, how much furniture you can buy. Beyond this, the only real limits are the living and comfort requirements of your family and your own personal taste.

If you have done your basic homework, you have already noted that there are no rigid formulas, either for living-room decoration or furniture arrangement. While certain floor plans deal more effectively than others with the special problems of space—long and narrow rooms, square interiors, living-dining areas, huge rooms, tiny rooms—even here one notices a new freedom of approach. Floating arrangements, angled arrangements, conversation pits, et al, point toward a freer manipulation of every kind of living space, easy or difficult.

It is at this point that you must reconcile personal style preferences with your life-style and entertaining needs. It's not as simple as it sounds; there are plenty of women who like to wear blue jeans one day and mink the next. Perhaps you own a family room or den that caters to your casual moments. If not, your living room will have to please the many "yous," so strike a happy balance.

If your living room is the only room the family lives in, make sure that you provide enough seating comfort, a place for the piano or storage for stereophonic equipment, if these are priorities, a spot for an intimate conversation, if you entertain on a small scale, plenty of traffic lanes if you give stand-up parties. Soil-resistant finishes and durable materials, as well as many easy-care furnishings, may also be important to you. If wall space is needed to display a personal collection of paintings, the furniture arrangement must take this into consideration.

Your choice of furniture placement, beyond satisfying specific living requirements such as those listed above, will also be another expression of your personal style. Using an angled arrangement rather than a more conventional way of handling the long and narrow syndrome demonstrates dramatically a preference for innovation rather than tradition.

Grouping furniture around a focal point continues to be one of the favored ways of arranging a living room. The focal point can be a natural part of the architecture—a bay window or window wall, a fireplace. Using a focal point to anchor the grouping creates visual interest and an appealing warmth and hospitality. This is why the real estate market puts such a premium on built-in, wood-burning fireplaces.

WILLIAM TURNER ASSOCIATES, INC.

A natural architectural element, such as a fireplace, gives focus to the conversational grouping. When none exists, a focal point has to be created. In this setting, a wide and handsome antique Coromandel screen serves the purpose. Cushiony sofas face each other across a super-sized plexiglass coffee table. Window wall is screened by full-length vertical blinds. Room designed by William Turner.

Create Your Own Focal Point

Lacking a natural focal point, you can always create your own. The possibilities are endless. It could be a large painting hung over a lacquered console table or chinoiserie cabinet. Or an antique armoire, a built-in bookcase wall, a cantilevered shelf or a modular system, Welsh cupboard, hutch, or tall secretary. The sofa itself can be effectively dramatized so that it becomes a focal point. Set the sofa in front of a Coromandel screen, or frame it with a pair of mirrored screens, or by two glass and chrome étagères.

Island, or floating, seating or conversation groupings are their own focal points by virtue of their position in the room. The grouping can be U-shaped or a partially open rectangle.

Lining up large sofas or cabinets against the long wall of a room tends to make it seem narrower; positioning such large pieces on the short wall visually widens the room. More than one furniture grouping will make a very spacious interior seem more intimate, but so will one large, floating conversation unit.

The long and narrow living room lends itself quite naturally to two separate groupings. If the room also has to serve a dual purpose—dining and living—then these two functions will determine where and how the division is made. Often one area begins where the other ends—such as a low serving cabinet for the dining area set behind a sofa that is placed at right angles to the wall.

Secondary Arrangements

Sometimes there is room in the existing space to create a secondary furniture arrangement in addition to the major grouping. The form that this takes is often determined by a specific living need—such as extra seating or a study corner—or by considerations of size and scale, such as using a large armoire to balance a dramatic fireplace grouping.

To establish the final furniture arrangement you will be experimenting with graph paper and templates, moving the templates around to form new groupings. If you still have to purchase most of your furniture, then you should also experiment with different sizes (of sofas or cabinets) as well as different kinds of furniture. Simply by altering the size of your sofa or by substituting a pair of love seats for one long banquette, you can develop a more efficient and attractive room plan.

Because of the emergence of seating modules, one has greater freedom in living-room arrangements, as these modules offer more flexibility. At the same time they can be less interesting than the traditional arrangement ploy of teaming a sofa with two comfortable chairs, as this latter arrangement allows for some diversity of style within the upholstery grouping itself. When working with seating modules, you often have to depend upon tables, desks, and other cabinetry to provide design character and personality.

Basic Priorities

As you work out the composition of your living room, you will automatically be answering certain basic requirements—the need for table surfaces to hold ashtrays, glasses, magazines, a tray of hors d'oeuvres, a tea service. A writing table, desk, or secretary will provide you with a study or writing area somewhere in the room; the first two designs are finished on all sides and lend themselves to a greater number of possible positionings within the area.

Comfortable seating should be designed to please a crowd or to encourage an intimáte conversation for two or three. There must be an attractive balance between upholstery and cabinet designs, between large and small pieces, short and tall ones. Avoid awkward combinations such as spindly end tables with clunky sofas, an oversized armoire for a boxy, pint-sized room.

Balance the Placement of Pattern

In allocating your fabrics, you may have styled the balance of pattern around a projected floor plan. If playing around with the templates changes the position of the sofa, or other major upholstered designs, you may also have to alter the fabric scheme. If the sofa is now closer to the draperies, it would be advisable to avoid a matching print, which would effectively throw all the pattern to one side of the room. A pair of chairs placed opposite the windows could be the new location for the print, with a plain texture designated for the sofa.

Backless furniture—benches, ottomans, and chaises—also promote arrangement versatility in the living room. This is especially helpful when there is one arrangement at the fireplace and another near the facing wall. By placing a chaise on one side of the mantel, you avoid the awkwardness of having one furniture design positioned with its back to another. Conversationalists can sit on either side of a large ottoman or chaise-shaped unit and talk to the people they face.

On your tour of model rooms, and especially decorator showhouses, you may have noticed the trend to build in an entire living room, either by the establishment of carpeted platforms or laminated perimeter shelving and storage, sometimes angled and sometimes parallel to the walls, but in all instances encompassing seating banquettes as well.

While this approach can maximize the use of space, create excellent additional storage, and personalize the architecture of a typical high-rise layout, it is usually expensive to install and not recommended for anyone who plans to move. It can also impart a certain blandness of line and material, as all the furnishings are designed to fit into each other comfortably.

Pull-up chairs, light tables, and furniture on casters gives the floor plan mobility and the decorative effect a much-needed change of pace. If you have already lived in one home, you have observed that your furniture gets rearranged whenever you entertain. Guests will pull one chair closer to another or to join a larger area when there are not enough people to fill up two separate conversation groups. This kind of flexibility is desirable—it adds to the efficiency of your living room.

Coffee Tables

The *sine qua non* of living-room design—the one kind of furniture style that is a top priority for almost every room—is the coffee table, even if coffee is served only in the dining room. The coffee table is a uniquely living-room design (although it is also used in other living areas such as den and family room), and it is often the selection that contributes the most effective or dramatic design accent.

The coffee table comes in just about every size and shape you can imagine. It is available in a host of wood finishes, as well as in colorful lacquers and laminates. Often the top is made of one material, the base of another. While twenty years ago coffee-table design was expressed primarily in only a few stereotypes—square, long rectangles, round and oval—today the variations go on and on.

These ingenious dividers give a family the option of using and enjoying this space as one large room or separating it into private activity areas. Furniture placement accomplishes some of the division; the rest is handled by floor-to-ceiling frames containing narrow venetian blinds that can be opened, closed, or pulled all the way up. Small-scale geometric carpeting, installed wall-to-wall, is a practical choice for a room that gets a great deal of use.

*Special and unexpected little touches can spell the difference between a
personal and conventional look. There are all kinds of delightful details
in this apartment living room, such as the straw lampshade, the pretty,
shirred treatment of the sofas' bases, the striped banding on the window
cornice, the huge floral painting, the unusual geometry of the wood and
glass coffee table.*

Now we see all-lucite coffee tables or designs that mix glass (the
top) with a plexiglass base. Plexiglass is often used for cubes; a pair of
these will serve as a coffee table. But cubes are also styled in wood
finishes, plastic and mirrored laminates, and are even fashioned entirely
from metal. The straight-lined Parsons table has become a ubiquitous
classic in coffee-table design; these are now being supplanted by "wa-
terfall" or scroll-shaped tables, also offered in laminates or lacquer but
featuring the softening accent of curves rather than hard edges.

Among the more popular coffee-table designs seen today are all lacquer tables, designs in painted finishes or decorative chinoiserie, the many, many interpretations of metal with glass, wicker with glass, and cylinders of plastic laminate, lacquer, or metal.

Lighter weight tables are favored for traditional interiors—such as the butler's tray and other tray-style designs. For country moods, coffee tables emerge as antique blanket chests, old or new trunks, large covered baskets, and low narrow wooden benches.

And in rooms where extra upholstery is critical, comfortable ottomans often do double duty as a coffee table—a large tray converts them to this purpose.

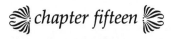

chapter fifteen

Dining Rooms

The dining rooms of the eighties may not be as architecturally imposing, as spacious, or as separate as dining rooms of the past, but they are certainly more decorative, more versatile, and more memorable. In the days when dining rooms wore a uniform—a matched complement of chairs, table, china cabinet, and server—most of these interiors were boring look-a-likes, and for that reason the most pedestrian rooms in the house. Today, even the tiniest dining area has style, a style that derives from a freer, more romantic, even a more dramatic approach to dining decor.

Which is as it should be. The dining room is not a hideaway for quiet reflection, for solitary pursuits. It is a gathering place for people, the members of the family, and occasionally their friends and guests.

A dining room should set the scene for conversation; it should offer a festive ambience for a gala dinner party or a holiday buffet. It can be pretty, lively, even a little *outré,* but never sterile and banal. It is your stage setting, the room you use to entertain, to play the host. The more interesting or mood-setting its decoration, the more festive and fun the event.

Of course dining must also be part of the family routine, but this can and should be enjoyed in an interesting and aesthetically provocative interior. Here is the room for marvelous wallpapers and fascinating paintings, a uniquely personal mélange of furniture designs or a wonderfully nostalgic expression of a bygone era. It's a room for a sumptuous oriental rug or a silken wall covering, for the visual excitement of the mix of unexpecteds—velvet with steel, glass with rattan, high-gloss lacquer with hand-hewn woods.

Dining-room decoration can also be super-serene and low-key, but this too can be expressed in subtle stylings that nonetheless reflect today's convention-free spirit. If it is part of a larger living area, it must of course relate to the style and color scheme of the major room but still provide a special ambience of its own.

What's Your Family's Life-style?

As with the other rooms of your home, you should design your dining room to fulfill the life-style requirements of your family, to deal effectively with the space and architectural assets and limitations of the area, and to coordinate with the general decorating style of your home.

And since the dining room serves a specific function, you should closely examine all aspects of this role. Will your family be dining there for three meals a day or utilize it only at dinnertime? Do you like to give sit-down dinners or prefer informal suppers? How much storage do you need for linens, silver, serving pieces? Must the room provide ample serving surface for buffet dining, and how many chairs will suffice?

The standard and matched complement of furniture, once favored for dining-room decor, was a simplistic approach, and as with most formulas, an easy one to implement. Today's more personal expressions require a great deal more planning, more imagination, and more skill. But the results are well worth the effort.

When Space Is Limited, Set Your Priorities

With space at such a premium, many families often convert dining rooms and areas into multipurpose interiors. In an apartment that contains no informal den or family room, the space of a generously proportioned dining room is sometimes divided into dining and sitting areas. The expanse of work surface offered by a dining table lends itself to the enjoyment of a hobby or homecraft—coin or stamp collecting, sewing, sculpting, the design of needlecraft canvases, photography, model shipbuilding; the list could go on and on.

Often an extra place is needed as a study area for a school project or work taken home from the office by either parent. If the dining room is used extensively for such a purpose, or even as a favorite spot for family games such as Monopoly and Scrabble, adequate storage should be provided here if possible.

After sifting through the role priorities of your dining room, you must then compose its style. Remember, you no longer have to, nor should you want to, utilize a totally matched package. Nor do you need to position the dining table in the center of your room, an approach once considered the basic format for dining-room arrangement.

Formal English dining room has a gracious yet understated elegance that derives from a glorious mix of glowing wood finishes, delicate crewel fabric used on host and dining chairs, Chinese export porcelains, oriental rug, and antique painting. Surprising eclectic touch: over-sized metal chandelier. Surface of the table is kept highly waxed so that no tablecloth or mats are needed to cover exquisite graining.

Favored classics, the lighthearted pedestal table, and wood, metal, and cane chairs, are popular choices for small dining areas. Placed near mirrored and window walls, this arrangement looks totally different although the same furniture is used in the dining area in one of the photographs in the color section.

Making the Floor Plan

In designing the floor plan for your dining room, first position your table and chairs, then decide how much wall space is available for serving pieces. Watch for a balanced arrangement, avoiding crowding large pieces into a small room or wedging a huge cabinet between two undersized windows. You can find enough lightly scaled dining furniture to satisfy every need.

Sometimes the architectural character of a room will give focus to the floor plan. A superb view of a garden or a city skyline might prompt the placement of the dining table near the window rather than in the center of the room. If space permits, the other side of the room could be converted into a small sitting area, or else a large cabinet could be used for balance.

Two separate tables—round and skirted or square and hard-edged— can change the tunnel vision of a long and narrow dining room. And sometimes traffic lanes are a problem; if so, you might try placing your dining table at right angles to one wall rather than letting it float.

Try to visualize the room as it would appear from the doorway—will the composition be pleasing and balanced? And while at the table, will the plan still be attractive and cohesive?

While many people prefer a separate dining room, because they can use it to evoke a more formal, private dining scene, others opt for the living-dining arrangement. Once this choice was prompted by economics; today it is often a meaningful solution to changing life-styles.

Current architectural forms, which often combine kitchen, dining, and living areas within a single open space, cater to the working wife and mother who does not want to be sequestered in a back kitchen while she prepares dinner. The open plan allows her to converse with her family in the living room or never to leave her guests as she goes back and forth to the kitchen during a dinner party.

In the past, room dividers, screens, and a deliberate arrangement of furniture was utilized to mark off the division of living and dining. This has become less important and less desirable; professionals like the change of pace provided by an open view of the different kinds of furnishings used in each area.

Variety of Mixtures

In doing your research, you have undoubtedly noticed that professional designers evoke interest and distinction in dining decoration by utilizing harmonious and compatible but nonmatching tables, chairs, and storage designs. They have also tried to introduce the softening element of additional upholstery whenever possible.

Mixing up finishes and materials while sustaining a similar style mood, or a purposeful mélange of disparate design genre, can make dining-room decoration express a more personal approach.

The ramifications and possibilities are endless; just leaf through a current issue of a popular decorating magazine to see a sampling of the new and individualistic design techniques. You'll see rattan and steel chairs with tortoise-shell finish Parsons-style tables, or a table with rich

Mix of furniture styles and finishes is responsible for the dynamic personality of this colorful dining room in a small city apartment. Sideboard offers generous serving space, also stores linen and flatware. Backgrounds are interesting too: cork-look wall covering and small-scale geometric carpet, installed wall-to-wall.

oak graining partnered with painted, bamboo-framed Chinese Chippendale chairs. Comfortable, fully upholstered chairs surround a sheet of glass atop marble pedestals, black Regency chairs are unexpected teammates for a modern pedestal table. A white-lacquered table gets Louis XVI chairs while bentwood designs pull up to a butcher-block pedestal table. Table frames are often of polished chrome, brass, and stainless steel; chairs too are framed in metal, generally tubular rather than flat. See-through glass tops, a favorite space expander, are supported by bases of metal, wood, plexiglass, carpeted platforms, wicker, and travertine. The versatile Parsons table, expressed in highly figured veneers, colorful laminates, lacquers, and painted finishes, is also favored because of the ease with which it partners period chair styles as well as modern seating designs.

Innovative Choices in Tables

Be sure to explore all the kinds of dining table designs as well as all the materials and combinations of materials. In addition to pedestal, or legged, tables, there are also trestle, harvest, butterfly, and skirted styles. For the inventive on a strict budget, or for those who do not want to invest in an expensive table that may be too small for the next home, plywood rounds with colorfully patterned skirts are a fine alternative. Another charming makeshift idea: a laminated shelf atop a pair of finished wooden or metal sawhorses.

Try for diversity in tabletop shape, especially if your storage pieces have hard edges. Oval, round, hexagonal, and square tables with rounded edges provide a needed variation.

Think also in terms of use and practicality when choosing a dining table. Glass tops do not stain but they can get water marks. Many new laminates that are stain- and spillproof come in wonderful wood-look textures or in graining that emulates marble and malachite. Manufacturers often use special finishes on wood tabletops to make them alcohol- and heatproof.

Sometimes the dining table is other than the long, rectangular stereotype. Two square tables, each with four chairs, provide a variation on the theme. When desired, the two can be pushed together to form one long design. Pairs or even multiples of skirted tables, circled with painted Queen Anne chairs, also offer versatility and the softening effect of added fabric and pattern.

Oval tables are often used, as are large rounds, a suitable selection when the dining room itself is square. In smaller rooms, or in areas where dining is a part of the living room, a charming ploy is the use of L-shaped banquettes with an oval or rectangular table plus several free-standing chairs. Country rooms combine a high-backed settee or a deacon's bench on one side of the table with ladder-back or spindle-back chairs on the other side.

Leg room is also of the essence in the smaller dining rooms, hence the use of traditional trestle and modern pedestal tables, which can accommodate more dining chairs comfortably than the leggy designs.

Tables that extend, that pull apart to receive additional leaves for additional seating, are always useful for larger dinner parties. A relatively new variation on the theme is to have console tables positioned against the wall that are the exact width and style as the dining table and can become an add-on when desired. This technique is an excellent way of extending glass and metal tables or sleekly lacquered designs.

EASTMAN KODAK COMPANY

A change of pace from the tried and the conventional is this dining arrangement that synthesizes comfort with style. Pillowed banquettes provide part of the seating around the brass-banded pedestal dining table. Wall hangings are framed photographs.

Chairs

There is no precise limit to the number or kind of dining chairs you can use. These may be all side chairs, all armchairs, or a combination of the two. Host and hostess chairs add comfort and glamour; because they are often pulled into the living room for extra seating, the additional cost of these designs usually pays for itself.

To soften the hard-edge geometry of dining table and storage units, fully upholstered chairs are often preferred. The comfortable host and hostess chairs now abound as multiples, providing dining-room decoration with an extra measure of luxury and comfort, encouraging family and guests to linger long after dinner is through.

In addition to wood veneers and painted finishes, chair frames are often made of metal or are fashioned from molded plastic. Wicker, rattan, and cane are featured on backs and seats; cantilevered metal bases, in the style first established by Marcel Breuer and the Bauhaus school, are popular choices.

Storage

Storage designs no longer follow the formularized concept—in many instances there simply isn't enough wall space for the once-standard china cabinet and server. Dining storage is now supplied by an armoire, a pair of étagères, a Welsh cupboard, or a laminated credenza. If a room is too narrow, three shallow bookcase cabinets that occupy much less floor space than conventional dining-room designs offer a lavish amount of storage potential. Open storage can also be built in, capitalizing on a recess or alcove; a long serving surface is established by a shelf cantilevered from the wall.

In many instances, the material used, or the finish selected for the storage design, is strikingly different from that of the table to avoid the curse of sameness. A brightly lacquered table might get a serving cabinet of richly burled veneers. An oak table is counterpointed with glass and metal étagères. The tall fruitwood armoire lends character to a sleek Parsons table and chrome-framed chairs.

Occasionally, an antique chinoiserie cabinet sparks a setting filled with contemporary dining furniture, a pair of curio cabinets, or an apothecary chest, replaces the more conventional hutch, or a lowboy squats under a series of shelves displaying collectibles. Corner cabinets, in wood or painted finishes, save on space and effect a built-in look; so do wall-suspended buffets.

Improvised Dining

In a house lacking a dining ell, a dining alcove, or some area within the living room, dining may have to be improvised. Often this is done in a foyer, where a large writing table does double duty at dinnertime, or a drop-leaf or extension console expands to accommodate a family meal. Bear in mind that the area should look like a foyer, that its dual-purpose character not be evident to the eye or this will spoil the sense of entry and introduction that a foyer usually provides. To improve the view, as a foyer usually lacks a window and natural lighting, treat the walls to a mural wallpaper, or turn the area into a mini-gallery of paintings and graphics. Don't crowd the space with too many chairs; at mealtime chairs can be pulled in from the living room or out from the closet where they have been stored. Regarding the latter option, there are many handsome folding chairs on the market today—such as lucite and metal designs, and molded plastic stacking chairs that are sleek space savers.

When dining must be established within the main living room, an area can be marked off by the furniture arrangement itself; often a sofa facing a fireplace at right angles to the wall will be the line of demarcation between dining and living. Another way to arrange for a living-dining room is to select, as your table, a piece of furniture that functions in ways other than for dining. For example, a large writing table, a standing game table, a skirted table, or even an oversized coffee table can all serve for dining, even though positioned as an integral part of the living-room decoration. And don't overlook the folding tables that can be whipped out of closets or wall units for instant dining.

One of the solutions of the past was the chair whose back folded down into a round table, and this is still a practical idea for a certain style of room, as is the traditional piecrust table whose top stands vertically when not in use. A tea cart can also be harnessed for intimate dining for two—the entire meal served on and from this handy piece of furniture. And don't overlook a bar as a dining surface in disguise, or even the generous-sized hunt table, that charming English design.

It goes without saying that the size and location of your dining room or area, and the basic design approach used throughout your home, will guide your selection of dining furniture.

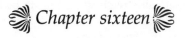

Chapter sixteen

Bedrooms

With so much focus on bedroom decoration these days, it hardly seems possible that at one time the bedroom was indeed at the bottom of the list. The home furnishings money went into rooms that counted, the ones that showed—living rooms, dining rooms—with just enough left over to provide a sleeping chamber with the bare essentials of a bed and storage. After all, no one saw it, so why bother?

Much has happened to change and redefine our approach to bedroom decoration. In the first place, we use our bedrooms so much more, and in so many different ways—for study, for reading, watching television, listening to music, as a sewing center, a library, an exercise studio, and—most important—as an adult getaway. With space at a premium, especially in smaller homes and apartments, there are no other special-purpose rooms, so the bedroom often has to serve a multitude of roles.

For this reason, we also shun decorating stereotypes. We avoid buying matched suites of furniture or typical "bedroomy" wall coverings. We experiment with fresh color ideas, unusual patterns, inventive window dressing, colorful pillowing. We mix finishes and furniture styles, choose inspired prints for our bed linens, and cover walls and tabletops with our most cherished collectibles. Nothing is banal or impersonal; everything is an expression of a very personal taste. No motel rooms for us, right in the middle of our own homes.

Of course we don't have quite the freedom in designing the bedroom as we do in the living areas of the house. Here there are priorities that must be satisfied. We must have a bed, ample storage space, and adequate lighting. And within the confines of what is often an ungenerous amount of space. Master bedrooms in some apartments that contain spacious living rooms are occasionally no bigger than a walk-in closet.

If you are staying in an apartment for only a few years, then it is wise to purchase bedding and storage that you will want to use over the long haul, even if this means a certain amount of modification for your present bedroom. You can stretch space on the bed wall, for example, by using a pair of wall fixtures or pharmacy lamps and eliminate one nightstand, or even both. There may be room in the adjacent living room for a marvelous armoire, and you can use this to store your out-of-season clothes, cutting down on the need for more than one dresser in the bedroom.

Your Floor Plan

Before deciding anything else, create a basic floor plan for the bedroom. Working with your graph paper, ruler, and templates, play around with all the possibilities. Perhaps you had wanted a king-size bed (the equivalent of two twin beds). Will it fit, and if so will it preempt some of the space needed for storage pieces? Can a queen-size be an acceptable substitute, or will you eliminate one storage piece and add more built-ins to your closet?

Before finalizing the position of the bed, take into account what other roles you want the bedroom to play. Placing the bed dead-center on the long wall, for example, may give you a lot of nice, open floor space, but no area large enough to contain a small seating arrangement. This would suggest placing the bed off-center, allowing ample space for whatever chairs or upholstered furniture you might want to add.

Unless space is no problem, you should also take special requirements into consideration before settling on all tables and storage designs. It might be necessary, for instance, to substitute a writing table or desk for one of the nightstands, or even to place the desk at the foot of the bed. In a narrow room, with a dearth of table surface, you might want to place a Parsons-style table next to the bed, running the long way (paralleling the bed).

Beds

The size of the bed will determine the size of the bedding. This is not the place to stint on quality; get the best quality bedding that you possibly can, with a mattress that is firmer rather than softer, for strong and lasting support. Quality box springs that will last a long time and hold their resilience are equally important.

Whatever your style preference, you can choose from a number of different kinds of beds. You can get a complete bed, with headboard, footboard, and side frames. Or just a headboard, to which you attach box spring and mattress on a frame or on legs. When twin beds attach to a single headboard, they are usually on frames with casters, so they can pull out for easy cleaning of the floor underneath.

In addition to conventionally shaped and styled beds, we now see much more of the platform bed. This can be a commercially manufactured design, a custom creation, or a built-in structure of carpeted plywood. Many platform beds are part of a built-in storage unit that swings around two walls of the room. One designer created a laminated platform bed, placed it in the center of the room with a unit containing nightstands at the head and a curved desk arrangement on the foot.

Those partial to the platform bed usually opt for a modern bedroom, complete with built-in storage and often room for a small exercise area. This kind of room also lends itself beautifully to a part-time home office, and to a freer, more flexible use of space, as the bed can often be placed in the center of the room or can simply float in any position that is desirable.

Probably no bed is more popular than the tester or canopy style—a design that literally dominates the decoration in both modern and traditional bedrooms. Contemporary versions of four-posters come through in chrome and brass, bamboo and rattan, in sleek, streamlined styling, and bed draperies and canopies are often added to an existing bed to create architectural interest and decorative impact. Large, paneled canopy beds, inspired by Jacobean, Early American, and French Provincial designs are also more popular today, offered in dark finishes or in the newly popular lighter stripped woods.

Storage Expanders

The usual complement of bedroom storage furniture is now available in an enormous choice of styles and finishes, often expanded by matching armoires, étagères, and bookcase designs. The tendency today, however, is to mix woods and finishes, often pale with dark, painted with stained, and occasionally to inject the added touch of a decorated design, a wicker table or chest, or a marvelously weathered antique.

Extra storage can also be "discovered" in the other furnishings you add to the room; a night table can be a small chest, two wicker trunks can finish off the foot of the bed or be placed in a small space of wall under a window. Or an ample amount of modular storage units can replace the usual combination of dresser and chest.

Mix and Match

Mixing styles, colors, finishes has become a more favored approach to bedroom decoration because it ensures a much more personal look than the anonymous effect of a lot of matched furniture. It is also easier to add another piece to an unmatched collection, often an important need when the family moves and has a larger bedroom. As long as the furniture styles blend easily or counterpoint successfully, there is no reason why you cannot do a certain amount of mixing, although it is advisable to seek some professional guidance if you intend to have a completely eclectic look. If you have been studying the mix-and-match bedrooms featured in magazines you will notice that the designer often uses generous amounts of a single pattern or print for draperies, bed covers, and so on, to orchestrate and integrate the composition.

A sweep of wall-to-wall carpeting, which is a preferred flooring treatment because it adds warmth underfoot, often essential to the "cocoon" quality of a bedroom, is also an integrating force in a room of mixed furniture styles.

As we mentioned in our chapter on living-room focal points, this is not a problem in the bedroom because the bed itself is so prominent that it becomes the visual focal point. Professionals like to use decorative devices to dramatize the bed, hence strengthening its role.

Canopies and Canopy Effects; Headboards

In addition to adding canopies to the ceiling that are partially extended or the full size of the bed, complete with matching or other bed draperies, designers will emphasize the headboard or create a headboard effect when none exists.

The possibilities are endless. An antique Persian painting on glass is placed at the head of the bed, or an oversized contemporary canvas. Lattice, purchased in a lumberyard and painted a color that contrasts with the wall hue, can be attached to the wall behind the bed and extend as high as the ceiling.

AREA RUG BY BIGELOW

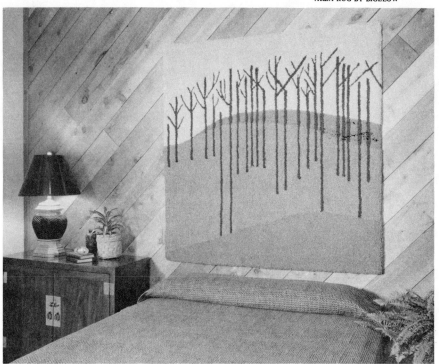

Great substitute as a headboard, and more decorative too, is this abstract landscape design executed in a custom rug. Pine planking, installed on the diagonal, provides a rich textural backdrop to the rug "headboard," a wonderful idea for a small bedroom.

The romantic four-poster bed, an abiding favorite, dominates a south-western-style bedroom, framed in rich tones of orange, and yellow with beige. The mix of seventeenth- and eighteenth-century-inspired English furniture is expressed both in pale and dark finishes. Small sitting-dining arrangement is positioned in front of glass doors that lead to an atrium filled with flowers.

One designer simply used a patterned fabric, matching the print of the spread, to sheathe the part of the wall behind the bed and over it. For a finished effect the fabric panel was edged with chrome strip molding.

A Colonial quilt is hung on the wall to serve as a headboard and often a short canopy is used—one that attaches to the ceiling but extends only about a foot or so from the wall. This style of canopy has one set of draperies that ties back at either side of the headboard.

Canopies do not always match the bedspread; sometimes their print merely reiterates the dust ruffle or a fabric on a chair. The canopy lining can match the carpeting or the accent pillows; the bed draperies can coordinate with the canopy pattern or be a lacy fabric.

Upholstered headboards are styled in traditional designs, in squared-off modern shapes, and more often, lately, in an arched or semicircular form, often tufted for an especially soft and pampered look.

Don't overlook the fabulous bookcase or storage headboards, a contemporary look that is a wonderful space expander, as it includes precious storage compartments along with table surfaces that serve as nightstands.

Another great substitute for a headboard is an admixture of pillows: large, rectangular, round, tiny, cylindrical. Their position is so orchestrated as to create enormous decorative interest at the head of the bed, as well as a charming and luxuriously romantic look.

Color

You can take your pick of color schemes for bedroom decoration. Soft pastels are still used, along with off-whites and beiges in monochromatic expression, but this approach is primarily for those who want a mood of restful repose. Others not only prefer the animation of lively prints but will surround themselves with brilliant wall color, sometimes a vivid red, a chrome yellow, or a parrot green.

Or they will use color for a dramatic effect, such as in a bedroom with high-gloss navy-blue walls, white laminated furniture, or dark chocolate-brown walls with white woodwork and pale furniture finishes. A bedroom utilizing a brilliant feather print will have bright-green carpeting and a lacquered bench of cerulean blue.

Windows and Walls

Sometimes the bed is set within an alcove and this alcove is side-draped and topped with a canopy that repeats the pattern and shape of the window valance. Window treatments can, of course, be executed in any of the possible materials and styles, but in the bedroom they tend to be more decorative than elsewhere.

Consistent with this more frilly or gussied-up look at the window is the oft-favored look of fabric-covered walls, sometimes applied fabric, occasionally shirred from pole to pole. This not only furthers the "cocooning" effect, but also intensifies a feminine look—a quality often preferred by men as well as women for the master bedroom. Dressed up with ruffled curtains, floral prints, a chaise longue, a pride of pillows and skirted tables—and of course a canopied bed—bedrooms are true boudoirs, with great romantically feminine appeal.

ETHAN ALLEN INC.

In the master bedroom of a prefabricated barn, bold, eye-stopping colors were needed to counterpoint paneled walls and wood beams. Vivid lime green of chair fabric and chrome-yellow carpeting take their cue from Matisse-inspired quilt. Brass and glass table, placed under the window, serves both as a nightstand and as a shelf for potted plants. Room designed by Edmund Motyka.

Spreads, Linens

No discussion of bedroom decoration could be complete without some mention of spreads and other bedcovers. While many designs are offered in full throws and fitted bedspreads, there has been a marked trend to the use of coverlets in combination with dust ruffles. Coverlets are lighter and easier to handle, and dust ruffles provide a permanent cover for bed frames, a popular support for much of today's bedding.

And, happily, so many bedspread, throw, coverlet, and dust-ruffle styles are offered in an assortment of ready-made sizes that it is not usually necessary to have them custom-made.

In recent years, the great pacemaker in bed dressing has been the patterned sheet, often designer styled, and offered in an extraordinary number of coordinates—comforters, dust ruffles, curtains and draperies, pillows, even towels. The rise of the designer-collection sheet program has inspired the emergence of the "undressed" bed, a great boon to the working woman or even the stay-at-home wife. No heavy bulky spread need be added; all that's necessary is a straightening up of sheets and comforter. At night there's nothing to remove, the bed is ready for use, as is.

Probably no single style has done as much to revolutionize the American bedroom as the high-fashion sheets. These wonderful sheets offer ready-made solutions to the exposed bed frame, present a whole world of pattern with which one can mix and match, and provide great widths of wonderfully printed fabric (king-size sheets) as yard goods to sew up a storm. Do-it-yourself with bedroom dressing has been so facilitated by these great sheets that many magazines and linens manufacturers offer comprehensive how-to-make-it booklets.

As many headboard designs are completely or partially (an exposed frame) upholstered, it is usually necessary to match the fabric used for it to the rest of the bed dressing. Often it is a simple matter of having sheeting of the desired patterns quilted and then covering the headboard with this, adding gimp if it is set within a frame.

Study, Snack, Exercise, and Hobby Areas

The mood you establish in your bedroom does not preclude the arrangement of special functions areas. You can create a study center, for example, in the sleekest or most romantic of rooms. All you need is

Once it was an unused bedroom closet, now it's one of the most frequented places in the house, a hobby center for a collector of shells. The changeabout was both simple and inexpensive. The clothes bar was removed and shelves installed. Doors were also eliminated and the same carpeting of the major area was continued into the new activity center.

a writing table, desk, secretary, or even a fold-down wall desk on which to work. This same arrangement can also be enjoyed as a breakfast table, a place for snacking while watching television. Informal dining can also take place within a small seating group, on a small coffee table placed before a love seat.

In shopping for seating furniture for the bedroom, be sure to look for smaller, more lightly scaled upholstered chairs that are especially good for rooms of modest proportions. Often such chairs come with swivel and rocking devices that broaden their use.

It is not surprising that the quest for fitness has often turned part of the American bedroom into an exercise space. Often a stationary bicycle is tucked out of sight on a wall next to a large storage piece, so that it is not immediately obviously a part of the decor. But in other instances an exercise center is an open arrangement, this usually occurring in a modern, platform, or built-in-bed arrangement.

Dressing areas are also included in many bedrooms, and once again this can be a secondary role played by the desk or writing table, or can be an arrangement specifically designed for making up and situated near the closet area. Excellent storage, a large mirror, and adequate task lighting are important requisites for such an area.

The best way to create a hobby or special activity center within the bedroom is with modular storage furniture that will not only contain some kind of fold-out or extension table but will provide enough storage space with which to organize and house all materials. This space-saving wall furniture is also an excellent option for creating a library area and television center, as upper units can be primarily bookshelves plus a special cabinet to house the TV.

Because the bedroom is such a private place, you can and should create whatever ambience is most pleasing to you, and establish whatever additional special purpose areas are necessary if your room is to play a round-the-clock role. But never forget that this is still a bedroom, and unless you also make it an extremely comfortable and pleasant place in which to wake up and fall asleep, you have not succeeded in providing for its more important service.

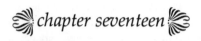

chapter seventeen

Children's Rooms

Children continue to display the same innocence, playfulness, and boundless supplies of energy that delight and exhaust us in much the same way that we did our parents when we were young. Yet our ideas about decorating a child's room have grown up enormously in a single generation. Today we try to satisfy a small fry's special needs, not our own; we strive to provide children with environments that are nourishing as well as comfortable and practical.

So, gone are the washed-out worlds of watered-down pastels, the Mother Goose decals, the cutesy decorating that once prevailed. We know now that even a young baby responds to vivid color, lively pattern, pleasing sound. Studies have shown that children react perceptively to the world around them, and we can nourish their sense of color and design, we can hone their innate good taste, by providing them with handsome and colorful interiors.

A Room for Many Uses

A child's room is more than a bedroom. It is his world, an indoor playground, a place to sleep, study, work, daydream—a place to be alone, to enjoy his own company. It is the room in which he stores his favorite things, first toys, then games, eventually records and sports equipment. And just as adults require an inner sanctum of their own, so do kids need a private hideaway—a spot to play with friends, real or imaginary, a place to be free because it's theirs.

Designing a child's room, according to the experts, is an ongoing process that has built-in flexibility, so that it is open to modification at the various age levels: infancy, preschool, school age, and teen age. This is accomplished by starting with a nucleus of furniture that can be expanded and added to as the child grows up. Backgrounds—wall coverings, window treatments, and accessories—are changed from age level to age level, adapting to growing and changing needs.

But at every age level there are certain priorities that are basic to the way we, and eventually our children (when they are old enough to participate), should plan these rooms. Wall coverings should be scrubbable, floor coverings stain- and dirt-resistant, fabrics washable and durable, and furniture hardy enough to withstand a great deal of wear and tear. Fragile materials are really not practical anywhere in a home with children, and they are decidedly out of place in a child's own room.

From the minute a baby rises on his haunches, he begins to stare at the bright colors around him. So even for this age level, provide interesting, even poster-bright colors in wall coverings, fabrics, and furniture. Instead of a nursery-style set of furniture, partner the crib with one or two dressers, simple in design, or possibly part of a modular system. You might want to add at least one child-sized chair, as he will soon be a toddler, and you can find a wealth of designs in stained or painted wood, in lighthearted wicker.

The Young Child's Needs

The preschooler needs more storage, especially shelf space for a growing collection of toys. This would be the moment to add upper open shelf units to those base cabinets already in the room. And there should be plenty of play space, if possible, for girls as well as boys. Since children are now beginning to develop a special sense of their own gender, and require different things from their room if they are boys rather than girls, be sure to gear the choice of pattern and accessories to meet this new awareness.

The preschool years are periods of enormous change and growth. And supercharged activity. You will be thankful that you invested in furniture with laminated surfaces or in wood cabinets with wood-look laminated tops. This is the time when he or she will graduate from crib to bed. In buying new furniture avoid anything with sharp edges and designs that will easily tip over. If you live in a cold climate, put an area carpet over the scrubbable vinyl floor that carries over from the infant's decor.

The schoolchild needs a desk, some hobby center, more storage space, task lighting, and of course some facility for overnight guests— another bed or a sleeping bag. Make sure that there is a comfortable but supportive desk chair; by giving serious attention to the business of homework you will be encouraging him to do the same.

Teen-agers' Needs

There should be no attempt to standardize teen-age decorating, any more than there should be an effort to categorize a teen-age personality. At this stage of life, children are as unique as their thumbprints, and their rooms should reflect their special qualities without the intruding discipline of parental ideas. Most teen-agers want to decorate their own rooms, and should be allowed to. If given a free hand, they will ask for your guidance and appreciate any practical assistance. Naturally, if a teen-ager comes up with something totally unrealistic or out of your budget, you will certainly make this clear.

In decorating a child's room you will approach the floor plan and furniture arrangement much as you would any other room of the house, with graph paper and templates in hand. If the budget is ample, you might want to hire a professional to create a built-in environment, but you can achieve similar looks with commercially made furniture, especially modular storage and platform beds. This could also be the room for which an enterprising home handyman could go to work. Magazines that feature decorating projects, and self-help books, are chock full of marvelous ideas that are remarkably easy to copy and install. Your child will certainly appreciate the extra effort expended on his or her behalf.

Children's Favorites

Certain kinds of furniture are especially favored for children's rooms as it appeals to their sense of adventure and romance: bunk beds for boys, canopy beds for girls. You can also be imaginative with furniture choices. A school-age boy would certainly enjoy a four-poster, if it's fashioned from rough-cut logs that are sold for fence posts and a frame for the mattress cut from 1 by 6-inch rails and a sheet of plywood. So would two sisters adore double-decker bunk beds, gussied up to emulate a canopied four-poster. Floor-length tie-back draperies, which soften the frame of the beds, are suspended from a shallow self-canopy attached to the ceiling. Also plenty of storage furniture with open shelving—it aids a child and encourages him in developing a sense of organization and prevents the frustration of "losing" possessions right in his own room. Shelved room dividers can also be positioned flat against a long wall to frame twin beds with architectural impact.

If wall space is at a premium, storage units, painted, finished, or laminated on all sides, can be positioned at the end of beds as tall footboards. Shelf partitions can be installed between two beds placed against a long wall; store books and games and mark the division of territory between two brothers or sisters in a shared bedroom. Or a cork-sheathed divider will create separate work areas as well as a place to post photos and artwork.

Speaking of artwork, make sure that there is plenty of hanging surface on which to display your child's efforts—pegboard, cork, even a fabric-covered wall.

Using your child's artwork as accessories in his room, much as you would display your own paintings or needlework pillows in the living room, will encourage him to continue, and also bolster his ego.

New Designs

A bumper crop of delightful furnishings designs, aimed to please the growing child, turns up in new introductions each season. One manufacturer has promoted a tubular bunk bed, with its ladder an integral part of the frame; another firm has offered a contemporary country version of the ubiquitous double-decker. One company has created a series of self-contained drawer units with their own covers that bunch to form a platform bed frame.

Not too long ago, a young couple, frustrated in their search for inventive, flexible, and attractive children's furniture for a city apartment, came up with their own line of knock-down elements that combine and attach to create any of the essentials of a child's room. Made from rigid, boldly colored vinyl tubes and wood boards, the units make bunk, loft, or trundle beds, adjustable shelves, desks, bulletin boards, dressers, and even movable posture chairs.

One designer has even invented a collection of play pillows that a child makes himself, using fabrics of his own choice and following easy step-by-step instructions.

A combination easel-blackboard telescopes to adjust to the various height levels of a growing child. The high-tech look of tubular metal frames an indoor gym, a desk and chair, even a bed. Many of the new, molded plastic chairs are a fine choice for a child's room, but don't overlook a relatively recent favorite—the versatile beanbag chair. And the many new versions of upholstered headboards, canopy and brass beds especially designed for a child's use.

Built-in storage maximizes the space potential of two children's rooms that were carved out of one large bedroom, now divided by partition and blinds. The baby's area has plenty of shelf space for toys and games, while the big brother's section has a similar complement of built-ins, these housing television, books, sports gear. A neutral, no-nonsense groundwork, a textured loop carpeting of Anso-X filament nylon, makes a warm and durable flooring.

For city apartments, architects like to design a single unit that serves all the needs of a child, and sometimes those of siblings in a shared room. Often this is a multilevel, multi-use construction attached to or placed against the wall and containing all the amenities for a child's life, even built-in lighting.

Gear the decorating scheme to the special interest of a child and that will automatically set the theme.

Make sure that there is ample shelf space for a child's collections—dolls, model airplanes, or ships, model cars, stuffed animals, books, records, etc. This could be provided by upper bookcase units, built-in shelves, or a wicker étagère.

One set of parents inventively cut out photographs of baseball players in action, had them blown up and mounted on the wall as a photomural.

In another instance, framed panels of a horse-themed wall covering were placed as a headboard design behind the bed in a dormer room for a young horse lover. As he grows, and his interests change, the wall covering can easily be changed to something else.

Windows

Window treatments should always coordinate with the style and theme of the room. For a tailored look, use window shades (laminated, painted, or stenciled), shutters, narrow Venetian blinds, vertical blinds, or fabric-covered panels. For a more frilly effect, any of the "adult" treatments scaled down—tie-backs, curtains, Roman shades, cafe curtains, etc. For the younger child, some kind of light-blocking shade or cover is needed for napping during the day, and older kids will appreciate this added element for sleeping late on weekends.

Using Color and Pattern

Color should be freely utilized for a child's decor, but allocated in such a way that it does not overpower it. If bold colors are chosen for the flooring and for fabrics, often the furniture is painted white. When the backgrounds are neutral and unpapered, bold and vibrant colors flourish on fabric prints and area carpets.

For one little girl's room, a vivid green, red, and yellow floral print was utilized in unexpected ways—to wrap the frame and posts of a tall four-poster, to cover a toy box underneath a window, and to slipcover a chair. For another girl's room, a lively print covers a daybed, makes tie-back curtains, covers miniature Louis XVI chairs, and becomes a skirted table—in a room that is otherwise entirely white.

Superflorals, bold plaids, zingy stripes, checks, and polka dots are especially effective motifs for children's rooms when expressed in oversized scaling and in eye-stopping color combinations. Or often color alone provides all the personality—combinations of brilliant blue with white, pink with red, yellow with orange, lime with lemon.

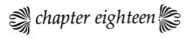

chapter eighteen

Kitchens

We've come a long way from baking bread in a beehive oven or cooling perishables with a huge cake of ice, but today's kitchens often impart the same kind of warmth and nourishment that made those kitchens of a generation or a century ago the heart of the home. Modern technology allows a kitchen to be more efficient than we ever dreamed possible. To have the best of both worlds we also endow them with the visual rewards of inventive decoration, enterprising storage, a masterful color scheme, a personal point of view.

Moreover, today's kitchen has really come out in the open. No longer closeted off in the rear of the house, it is often central to family life, a place where everyone cooks and congregates. Even guests enjoy participating in the preparation of a meal in what has become one of the most appealing and attractively designed rooms of the home.

All of this is part of changing life-styles. The disappearance of servants and the emergence of the working-wife-mother have forced a virtual revolution in kitchen design and planning. So even the most up-to-date cooking center, complete with microwave oven, trash compactor, food processor, and every other gadget designed to facilitate food preparation and cleanup, is often a fascinating and inviting interior.

Much of this has been made possible by the development of new materials such as laminates, now offered in a fabulous choice of colors, wonder surfaces such as marblelike Corian, and the utilization of ceramic tile for counter tops, backsplashes, walls, and floor. Appliances are sprayed in bold, trendy colors or have front panels that can be color-cued to the prevailing scheme or made from the same material as the cabinets. And manufacturers of stock cabinets proffer not only a wide variety of wood and laminate finishes but welcome feats of engineering that help simplify the organization of storage. To enhance all of this are lighting ploys such as the addition of a skylight or luminous ceiling, the installation of ample downlights and under-counter fluorescents, even the add-on of a window wall or a greenhouse alcove.

A simple "cosmeticizing" job—a freshening up of an old kitchen—does not require elaborate planning. Here a simple refinishing or repainting of cabinets, the installation of new counter tops, appliances, flooring, and wall covering may be all that the budget allows.

Try to get as much mileage out of such a limited re-do by selecting materials, designs, and color ideas that will give your kitchen a really fresh look, although the changes have been minor. Avoid typical or kitcheny wallpapers, replace your old vinyl floor with a durable one of ceramic tile, use one of the new counter-top materials or colors, add track lighting where feasible or replace the old fixtures with smashing-looking contemporary ones. A new wall clock that emulates an antique shape or is an innovative modern design will also enliven your kitchen. So will grids or pegboards hung with assorted pots and pans, or the ubiquitous ceiling rack, also for pots and pans, a handy idea borrowed from restaurants.

Add framed prints or posters if you have enough wall space; replace a discolored and dated wallpaper with a sleek modern graphic in easy-to-keep-clean vinyl. Remove the faded tie-back curtains and install vertical blinds or acrylic shelves to support a bevy of potted plants. Spruce up old cabinet doors with wall covering or, as one designer did, with photo blowups sealed with polyurethane. Create a photo gallery of family pictures over a breakfast table pushed against the wall. And if replacing the counter tops is beyond your budget, "face-lift" the old ones with a stunning waterproof wall covering.

Recessed or strip lighting installed under the upper cabinets will also make a difference in terms of how well your kitchen functions. A new set of country-style or contemporary canisters is also a quick and inexpensive way to give your kitchen a new spirit. But don't make changes in a random manner. Think in terms of the kind of look or style you want to create, just as if you were starting from scratch, and then make whatever changes you can afford that will accomplish this.

In the partial or radical process of remodeling, function must dove-
tail with form, and both must express in the best way possible the special requirements and living styles of the family. Of course it makes
more sense to remodel a kitchen in a house or apartment that you own
rather than rent, as you will be enhancing the resale value of your
property. Occasionally a renter will remodel his apartment, but usually
this is because he anticipates staying for a long time and has the full
cooperation and consent of his landlord.

Cheerfully Cluttered or Smoothly Streamlined

Are you an everything-in-its-place kind of cook or do you prefer the
charm and clutter of the let-it-all-hang-out look? Very possibly your
basic style is somewhere in between, but whatever the preferred effect,
you can still provide your kitchen with efficient and organized storage.

For the neatness freak are all of the various kinds of storage units
now available in stock cabinets, plus drawer and cabinet organizers
that can be put within existing cabinets to make them store even more
efficiently. Compartmented utensil holders, racks that screw onto cabinet doors, double-decker plastic units that store spices and other small
jars, swivel designs, wire-rack spin shelves and pull-out baskets, metal-
lined and covered drawers for breads and other staples, a roll-out shelf
for trash baskets, pull-up hinged shelves that store small appliances
behind closed doors are among the many handy devices that maximize
interior storage and keep counter tops clutter free.

By the same token, country clutter can have a method to its
madness. What initially appears to be a flight of fancy may in fact be
an unexpected but effective way to store. The fact that so much is on
view does not make it less efficient. Racks hang from ceiling and beams
to support a collection of pots, colanders, baskets, and large utensils.
Ironstone pitchers and ceramic crocks collect assorted wooden spoons
and wire whisks. Wine racks stand free on a counter or are installed
beneath some upper cabinets. Hanging wicker or wire baskets hold po-
tatoes, onions, oranges, fresh vegetables. Old-fashioned canning jars
are converted into useful canisters and grouped on an open shelf. In
addition to a complement of cabinets, often a free-standing piece of
furniture (if space permits) such as a Welsh cupboard or hutch of
stripped pine displays a collection of prized pottery. Plate rails and
spoon racks abound.

Short on space but big on style and storage potential is this streamlined apartment kitchen utilizing sleek white cabinets. Pale cabinet pulls reiterate the soft tones of inlaid butcher-block counter tops.

Bands of contrasting color on drawer and cabinet fronts create a luminous graphic effect in a buff and poppy-colored kitchen by Dexter Design, Inc. All surfaces are Formica laminates. Wood plank-style flooring extends from the kitchen into the adjacent greenhouse dining area.

Cabinet Diversity

At one point, beautiful, well-engineered, and meticulously fitted kitchen cabinets were available only as custom designs. Today, manufacturers of cabinets offer enormous style diversity—to appeal to the most tidy or most country-clutter oriented of cooks. These come through not only in a wide choice of materials, colors, and finishes but also in the kind of cabinet. These stock designs are now fitted with their own pull-out and partitioned drawers, with concealed cutting boards, lazy-susan pantry units, swing-out shelves for additional deep storage, turntables in corner units, pull-out dining tables, tall cabinets to store vacuums, brooms, mops, and other supplies.

Cabinet materials today, for stock as well as custom qualities, include such woods as maple, pine, oak, walnut, cherry, pecan, ash, redwood, cedar, even barn siding, as well as plastic laminates in a wide range of wood-look textures and a rainbow of fabulous colors.

Counter Tops, Backsplashes, Work Islands

Also contributing to the greater self-expression in kitchen design are favored counter-top and backsplash materials once limited to plastic laminates. Plain or patterned ceramic tile in standard or mosaic sizes, stainless steel, marble, Corian, a solid synthetic that looks and feels like marble and is extremely durable, and butcher block, a popular choice for country kitchens, and even copper are used as frequently as the laminates, which now come in such an expanded range of colors and textures.

If you have assembled a portfolio on kitchens, as with other rooms of your house, you have undoubtedly been fascinated and surprised by the versatility of kitchen design.

A modern kitchen, converted from the dining room of an older house, may be composed exclusively of work islands, laminated in bold red, or might be an unexpected theme of black, white, and steel, or white, lacquer blue, and lucite. An all-white kitchen can be relieved of hospital sterility by a series of colored enamel sinks, or by a ceiling of bold wallpaper graphic, or by a floor of handmade terra-cotta tiles.

Designers love to play around with laminate colors, sometimes combining two citrus hues, such as lemon and lime or lemon and orange—and then apply them Mondrian style, sometimes on upper cabinets, sometimes on base cabinets.

For a supersleek effect, metal-glint laminate cabinets are combined with mirrored backsplashes, or such backsplashes are utilized for a kitchen whose walls, cabinets, and counter tops are painted a deep purply pink.

Chopping blocks and work islands also become designers' *tours de force*. A chopping block will be encased within a cylinder of steel, and work islands feature not only protruding snack counters but often unusual shapes—oval, hexagonal, or angled—that are more interesting than the conventional rectangles.

Such islands abound in today's kitchens, whether of the supertidy or country-clutter variety. Some of these islands are even portable; others are so comprehensive they even include built-on towel and magnetized knife racks, hooks for cutting boards, and electrical outlets for appliances. Many contain sinks or cook tops.

If there are two active and energetic cooks in the family, the kitchen can accommodate this, often including smooth and conventional cook tops or a new or revamped restaurant stove that can contain as many as three ovens, a warming oven, and eight burners.

Today's kitchen can be straight out of a New England farmhouse, a Norman cottage, or a space-age environment. Each and all is possible with the variety of cabinet styles at one's disposal.

Variations in Color and Material Application

Color knows no limit. A kitchen may be radiant in blue cabinets, white counter tops, and peach walls, or offer the sophistication of glossy brown cabinets and walls and taupe ceramic tile for counter tops and flooring. One kitchen will be inspired by European fashions and feature white cabinets framed with natural wood. A country kitchen will take the natural look even further with cabinets that are unpainted and unstained, protected only with a clear sealer.

Materials are used in unexpected ways. Yellow ceramic tile on the ceiling creates a sunny kitchen, brick-colored tiles climb the side of a rounded work island. Decorative Portuguese tile faces cabinet doors, or a laboratory material, such as black Alberene, becomes the surface for a pastry-making center. Vinyl sheeting, with woodlike graining, is installed for a parquet-look floor. A rectangular rack, suspended over a cooking island, supports lighting fixtures as well as baskets and pots. Or bleached-white, rough-hewn cedar panels face the sides of a circular cooking island.

Sometimes the cabinets, counters, and backsplashes are of matching laminates to create a monochromatic effect. But occasionally two or more laminate colors are mixed or juxtaposed. For a change of pace, the counter tops and backsplashes will be of different hues. A contrasting color on upper drawers of base cabinets will create a graphic design that sweeps around the entire area. For a playful look, half of a side-by-side refrigerator is yellow, half is white.

Or all of the cabinets will be white, except for the work island, counter tops, and backsplashes of sunny yellow. Or a small galley will be a masterpiece of pale gray, stainless steel, white, and butcher block.

A Mix of Moods

Occasionally, kitchen design strikes a balance between country clutter and contemporary flair—mixing natural woods with white ceramic tile and grid-patterned wall covering. And for a stark effect, a floor of slate tile, almost black in appearance, will underscore a white kitchen with strategic touches of red.

Yesterday's popular wall organizer—pegboard—is still used, but more and more frequently this is being replaced by the high-tech wall grid for contemporary and country kitchens alike. Available in any size, to be sprayed any color, these metal grids are marvelous space stretchers in tiny apartment galleys where they can harness any unused slice of wall.

Often a kitchen is a compromise of clutter and concealment, mixing base cabinets with open shelving or open shelf cabinets on upper walls. To accomplish this look without the need for constant dusting, one designer asked a restaurant supply firm to custom-make steel-framed cabinets with glass doors. Suspended from the walls, these evoke the same look as completely open storage but have the practical advantage of dust protection.

Another interesting device is the cabinet door that opens to reveal an interior devoid of shelves but with a pegboard lining from which are hung all the small cooking utensils.

Another clever convenience is a drawer of spice jars laid out on their sides for quick identification, or a slanted pantry shelf from which canned goods are removed from the bottom, ensuring the proper rotation of storage; new cans are placed at the top.

No longer are the recesses over the cabinets filled in. The open tops become receptacles for baskets, colanders, oversized pots, and cookware. In a high-ceilinged room, often a galleried shelf stores and displays baskets, serving accessories, and collectibles.

In order to enhance the amount of natural light available, most kitchen windows, no matter what the design approach, are left uncurtained. At most a row of glass or lucite shelves will hold potted plants, a collection of miniature dolls. As we have mentioned earlier, skylights are often added, and overhead fixtures and downlights combine with under-counter fluorescents to provide general and task illumination that prevents the cook from working in her own shadow. Track lighting also flourishes as a popular kitchen device because it offers flexible task lighting, often a top priority in an active kitchen.

YORKTOWNE CABINETS

Pale oak cabinets, rich terra-cotta ceramic tile, and gleaming white, marble-like Corian counter tops provide a sleek but charming country look in a remodeled apartment kitchen. Narrow blinds repeat the blue of geometric vinyl wall covering used on walls and ceiling.

ALLMILMO ZEILOPLAN JAPAN BEIGE KITCHEN

Compactly designed kitchen provides a dining counter supported by nautical ropes. Handsome wood-look cabinets are surfaced with a durable laminate. Soffits and suspended shelf offer ample extra storage area, while ceramic tile, which sheathes floor and backsplashes, introduces a darkly dramatic counterpoint to the warm wood tones.

A word should be said about cabinet hardware in stock designs, which are as varied as the cabinets themselves. Pulls protrude or are recessed and are made of brass, rosewood, white porcelain, decorated porcelain, colored plastic, see-through acrylic, and black iron, to name a few. Stock cabinets now feature magnetized catches on doors (this used to be limited to custom work), which allows for quiet opening and closing of doors.

As the kitchen emerges as a marvelously efficient and handsome working arena for every member of the family, it is not surprising that more and more appliances and gadgets are included. In addition to doubling up on sinks and cook tops, new kitchens include self-venting barbecues, rolling wine racks and serving carts, recessed toasters, and devices borrowed from restaurant design.

Now you see it now you don't. A woven shade pulls up or down to reveal or conceal a kitchen in a small studio apartment. Raised platform, added to living area, lets the mirrored divider counter serve for dining. A pair of wall fixtures illuminates the counter area.

Track lighting provides task illumination in an informal kitchen with country-style cabinetry highlighted by wrought-iron hinges and white ceramic pulls. Easy-keep flooring is ceramic tile. The decorative clock and framed prints are among the few wall accessories in a room that is kept clean and functional.

Ease of use and comfort are also important considerations. Wall ovens can be installed side by side instead of piggy-back; the dishwasher set on a raised level if the members of the household are very tall.

It is easy to see how today's kitchen connects with ease to adjacent living or dining areas; the same "nonkitcheny" materials chosen for the working spaces can be continued into the living areas.

As we explore the foreign worlds of ethnic and exotic cooking, we ask our friends to share the experience, even help with the work. Our new blossoming collection of tools and materials—woks, processors, pasta and yogurt makers, racks or suspended clumps of drying herbs—all can be harnessed along with the basic elements of kitchen decoration to make this room as personal and varied as we might wish.

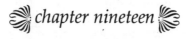

chapter nineteen

Family Rooms

The family room is a relatively new kind of room, born a generation ago, sprouting coast to coast as part of the housing explosion, the baby boom, indoor-outdoor living, casserole, and barbecue dining. No builder dared to exclude it; an overnight sensation, the family room became the star attraction of real estate ads and tract development brochures. Different from the "finished basement," a recreation or rumpus room located below deck, the family room adjoined or extended from the kitchen. As one wall faced the patio or terrace, the need for easy access and an ample view gave rise to the sliding glass door, a feature that was to become synonymous with family-room design.

Magazines heralded the new "togetherness," urging families to enjoy their own company, on vacations, in their own backyards, and most especially in the family room. Shaggy and tweed carpeting, rough-hewn furniture, childproof fabrics, shelving systems, and modular storage units came into their own as the word went out for furnishings that could stand the wear and tear of family activities, the advent of buffet dinners, televised football, child-oriented households.

Today's Family Room

Nothing has really changed that much since, but the decoration of the family room has naturally matured over the years and has expanded its role to incorporate facilities for stereophonic systems, hobby centers, home offices, and elaborately equipped cooking centers. The cliché-ridden blueprint for family-room decoration has been replaced by a fresh and personal approach that is compatible with the family's specific requirements and its own design and style preferences. While durability and ease of care are still top-of-the-list priorities, the overworked family-room banalities of leather-look vinyl and checkerboard tiles have pretty much disappeared.

Nor is the family-room feature a special pride of newer housing. Owners of older homes are developing such areas for themselves, either by adding on or by reclaiming such rooms as attics, porches, basements, car ports, garages, spare bedrooms, and oversized but obsolete kitchens.

Even more significant are the brand-new architectural concepts that merge the functions of living rooms and family rooms, providing one large and open area in which all the dining, cooking, and living activities take place.

This is not only the case in innovative modern structures but in newly revived and often remodeled structures such as farmhouses, barns, and revamped city brownstones. The sweep of space provided by such homes is often two stories high, with bedrooms tucked away in lofts or on balcony levels.

Today's new family room not only encourages family gatherings but nourishes the generation gap in the healthiest of ways by providing, in tandem with the living room, two separate living spaces, so that teenagers and parents can enjoy friends or special interests without impinging upon each other.

No two family rooms are or should be the same, any more than two families can be identical. The shape and architectural style of the room will also encourage a more personal expression.

If an unused or antiquated part of the house is being reclaimed as a family center, specific considerations should be kept in mind. If an attic area is to be converted from a catchall of outgrown tricycles into a beautifully paneled family area, focus on lighting. This may require the additional expense of opening up a skylight, a worthwhile investment. A former basement should not only be given adequate illumination but furnished with materials that will withstand dampness, as well as new walls or paneling to conceal pipes and wiring.

Recycling a garage may entail removal of the doors and the installation of a fourth and windowed wall. If the room, wherever located, is to be a music center, favor accoustical materials on walls and ceiling, wall-to-wall carpeting, and lined curtains. Make sure that there are doors with which to isolate the sounds of music from the rest of the house.

Planning and Decorating

Planning a family room of any size, shape, or location requires you to "pencil in" with paper and templates your needs in order of importance. Usually you will be establishing one major seating group that is both extensive and comfortable. Other areas or activity centers will then fall into place, according to logic and the limits of space. Obviously a dining area will be positioned closest to the kitchen, a pottery or painting center nearest to natural light.

A hearth is the natural place for the conversation grouping, a long wall the obvious receptacle for a storage system. The television should be conveniently placed, stereo speakers properly separated. Your own patterns of family living will suggest other accommodations as well, such as a permanent game table for bridge or puzzle buffs, a built-in screen for watching home movies, a music corner for family jam sessions.

Stain-resistant finishes and carpet fibers, high-fashion colorations in plastic laminates make it possible to express a variety of style moods while still ensuring practicality. While many will opt for casual, informal textures, low-key colors, a "laid-back" look, others may want a prettier more decorative style, even in family areas. If the room faces a garden, for example, animated, spring-fresh fabric prints, lighthearted wicker, and glass-topped tables can generate a blossom-bright, outdoor style.

A serious art collector wants understated but not necessarily supercasual backgrounds that will let his paintings take the spotlight. For a romantic look, tailored to practical needs, a family chooses mirrored tables, colorfully painted wicker chairs, an oriental rug, white ceramic-tile floor, paisley, and lucite.

Shelving—built-in, wall-attached, or free-standing—can house books and stereo equipment but also display a collection of folk art or earthenware.

Favorite choices for family-room seating are various styles in modular seating or else built-in banquettes—both encouraging the kind of large-scale conversation so often enjoyed in this kind of room. If guest facilities must also be provided, a pair of sofas, one a convertible, is often a popular alternative.

Country Look

Country decorating, an approach that celebrates the rich and simple pleasures of rural life, that embraces country-house comfort as well as clutter, is an understandably appealing style that can be easily articulated in a combination of living, dining, and kitchen areas. Based in a remodeled barn or a city townhouse, this exuberant country style expresses itself in siding-covered walls, brick hearths, hand-decorated tile, sisal rugs, basketry, stripped-pine armoires, whitewashed walls, shutters, lively small-scale prints, quilts, and Colonial collectibles. From the kitchen ceiling is suspended every kind of wonderful cooking utensil, pot, and butter mold, bunches of dried corn or drying herbs.

If the family action center is also a part-time disco, provide for enough smooth and open floor space, use movable furniture (on casters). As a second living room that takes on the overflow crowd of frequent parties, the family room can use the quick extra seating offered by assorted stackables.

The essential principles of the Early American keeping room—a gathering place where all family activities took place, and where the fire was "kept," so that it never went out—are being revived today in both contemporary and traditionally country housing. Architects favor the arrangement because the same space occupied by three undersized rooms can be opened up for the one free-flowing great room. For working mothers who hate being shut off in the kitchen during precious hours with their families, for weekenders who enjoy participating in assorted family activities, these new great rooms have obvious appeal.

In the process of remodeling or adding on, walls are removed, space is juggled, original areas juxtaposed as more space is added to the pot. Dispensing with interior walls makes it all seem so much larger; rearranging the space makes it work more efficiently. The additive of so much vertical space, both in reborn barns and in modern structures, has dramatic impact; double-decker and clerestory windows, skylights, as well as many and taller windows, enhance natural lighting.

Exposed brick walls, paneling of every wood and finish, beams, and most especially hearths or fireplaces are conspicuous by their presence in new family or great rooms. Effectively defining the living area within the wide-open space, the fireplace anchors the conversation grouping, which should be warm and intimate enough for only two to enjoy.

TREND CARPET/AMERICAN OF MARTINSVILLE

Country-cozy rooms continue to be abiding favorites; they offer comfort and casual relaxation and a delightful bucolic flavor. Here the country style is expressed in a living room that mixes colorful prints and patchwork with textured white Herculon fabric. Fool-the-eye random plank floor is actually patterned carpeting.

Great Rooms

The mushrooming of these new great rooms, family areas, superliving spaces—call them by any label—is not expressive of a return to the togetherness syndrome of the fifties or a device exploited by builders to sell houses. It is prompted by a need to use what has become a most precious commodity—space—as inventively and efficiently as possible. It also reflects the changing role of the home itself. Technological advances such as sophisticated sound systems, wide-screen and play-back television, Home Box Office movies, uninterrupted by commercials, make it very easy for Americans to entertain themselves at home. Elaborate cooking centers, often outfitted with a double complement of sinks, cook tops, ranges, and processors encourage culinary adventures *en famille*.

It's easier to stay at home; it's also safer and far less expensive, when one considers the cost of a movie, a restaurant meal, a gallon of gas. So the family living space, which most accurately describes these new arrangements, promises to continue an effective answer to challenges of the eighties.

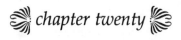

Bathrooms

They say that history repeats itself. Nowhere is this more in evidence within our own homes than in the bathroom, which reexpresses in contemporary American terms the same principles of luxury, pampered comfort, and bodily fitness so celebrated in the baths of ancient Rome. Of course these principles have been expanded and amplified by modern plumbing and technology, and by concepts borrowed from other cultures—the sauna from Finland, the hot tub from Japan—as well as that here-to-stay American institution—the spa.

But the bathroom of the eighties is not just an exercise in sybaritic pleasures or a fitness parlor; it is also an attractive and personal living space, as much a part of the interior landscape as any other area of the house. Gone are the typical "bathroomy" accessories and materials, the clinical and sterile decorating, the forgettable wall coverings, and the naked light bulb. Bathrooms are more often than not comfortable and beautiful sitting rooms and dressing areas in which one is never startled to see a cushiony chaise, a bergère, a painted antique dresser, a gilt-framed mirror. A luminous ceiling, a skylight, built-in downlights, or flexible tracks provide dramatic and useful general and functional lighting. A mini-garden flourishes near and around the tub or the sliding glass doors of a flower-filled patio or fills a greenhouse window.

Old favorites such as ceramic tile are not relegated to the sickly tones of pale green, pink, or blue. They are used in every color of the rainbow, and in decorated Mexican and Portuguese designs. Other natural materials, such as marble and onyx, slate, travertine, brick, and specially treated wood, share the spotlight along with laminates, colorful vinyls, and marblelike Corian. Bathroom fixtures are now offered in the sleekest of modern styling or in fresh adaptations of period designs, running the gamut from elegant brass and painted porcelain to svelte shapings in chrome and steel.

WASHBASIN AND FIXTURES BY SHERLE WAGNER INTERNATIONAL

Old World touches and modern plumbing team up in a bathroom mixing Victorian nostalgia with contemporary ingenuity. Designers Irvine and Fleming created this interior featuring a Victorian-style china washbasin, a floor of flowered ceramic tiles, and an appropriately feminine window treatment.

op) *The dramatic con-
st of dark paneling
th rough plaster walls
s the scene for a living
om whose Far Eastern
ood derives from the
x of exotic fabric
nts, oriental rug, and
sorted artifacts. For
ded drama, ceiling
ams were painted a
yal blue. Designed by
dmund Motyka.*

(Left) *Muted browns plus
white give a warm and
space-enhancing style to
narrow galley kitchen.
Brick-look vinyl flooring
is used for dining area
also, adding to the flow of
space. Note the pale wood
lattice screens at windows.*

(Right) *A dull or ne-
glected corner can weaken
the visual impact of an
otherwise attractive and
interestingly furnished
room. Dramatic corner
strategy, conversely, will
add immeasurably to a
room's enrichment. Here
it's done with an antique
Coromandel screen, a
round table wrapped with
a tassel-trimmed skirt, and
an elaborately carved
Louis XV chair.*

Chrome-yellow walls and floral chintz set the stage for a romantically eclectic room featuring a harmonious mix of wood and painted finishes and the surprise of a contemporary-style, angled furniture arrangement. Designer Richard Neas indulged in the sparkle of hothouse colors and in an interesting play on texture—chintz, wool, velvet, and fur.

(Top) The magic of color can go a long way, even when space is sparse. This dynamic scheme of red, white, and black turns a nondescript entry hall into an exciting area. Designer Edmund Motyka counter-pointed bold geometric wall covering with black-and-white checkerboard vinyl floor.

(Bottom) Once a breezeway, now it's a colorful activity center for a multiplicity of hobbies and crafts. Yellow modular cabinets offer plentiful storage in an amazingly compact manner. The plastic tops of these units make a wonderfully practical surface for potting plants and flower arranging.

*A romantic strategy for dining in a small space is executed in marble and steel by designer Robert Metzger. **He has arranged for diners to face an explosion of pinks in an oversized modern canvas** rather than a blank wall, always a problem with against-the-wall dining. Unusual and dramatic tabletop accessories also compensate.*

Personal Looks in Bathroom Decor

The decoration of the bathroom is, as with any other room, a matter of personal preference and style. As fixtures now come in many high-fashion shades, this will broaden the options, but you can also introduce fascinating color in counter tops, cabinets, flooring, wall covering, curtains, towels, and accessories. The only limitations here are practicality and safety; be sure to use materials that can withstand dampness and humidity.

The popularity of saunas has spread the wood look throughout the rest of the bathroom—an obvious choice for the natural or country-style approach. It is not unusual to see walls, ceilings, and cabinetry, even the sides of island tubs, made of cedar, barn siding, oak, even rosewood—materials that have been sealed and protected against the rigors of the atmosphere.

Professionals demonstrate that a little imagination can go far toward creating a very individual look. Patterned tile, or tile inlaid in interesting geometric juxtaposition, matte-finished, or glazed, or a brick-look texture can also be very striking. Hand-painted basins, counter tops made of malachite, lapis, and tiger's eye are other, often costly elements to ensure a special style, usually worth the extra investment in the long run.

Shower curtains are conspicuous by their absence in many of the newer bathrooms. They have become less important as stall showers, often in combination with steam baths, are offered as free-standing units. These contain a folding door, contoured seat, storage compartments, and a hand spray. Another gadget that has obviated the need for curtaining is the hand-held or telephone-style shower spray, which permits a more flexible adjustment of water direction.

A comfortable, deeply cushioned chair, traditional or contemporary, patterned or plain, belongs in the bathroom too, if space permits. These can be completely upholstered, made of wood or wicker, or even be exquisite antiques. Other free-standing furniture, such as tables and chests, can provide character and enrichment as counterpoints to sleek built-ins. So can a painted cabinet with upper shelves to display a personal collection and lower storage for linens and lingerie.

A Victorian bamboo magazine rack, a modern desk with chair, a country French armoire, to handle the overflow of bedroom storage, are all possible bathroom selections.

Washable floral-stripe wall covering and latticed framework above stall shower and over the window provide a high-ceilinged bathroom with two closely related diamond-shaped patterns that provide the interior with its decorative interest. Vintage wicker table and rocking chair are charming accents.

Graphics and prints can accomplish wonders in the bathroom—adding visual interest, warmth, and individuality. And this might be just the place for a gallery wall of prized family photographs. Perhaps your black thumb will turn green if you house plants in the damp climate of the bath near the light of a large window.

Every kind of look is favored these days in bathroom decor—from slickly high tech to country cottage. Even the posh glamour of the thirties is expressed in counter tops of mirrored mosaic tile or a dressing room lit by theatrical makeup bulbs. Some designers enjoy the surprise of old mixed with the new. A modern bathroom gains instant character by the addition of weathered beams to a sloping ceiling or by a polyurethane-finished oak floor and paneling. An antique country cabinet is even more fascinating with its contemporary basin and modern fittings.

Open shelving is utilized in quantities for bathroom decoration—to hold plants, books, extra towels, accessories. It was used as a space divider by one designer who created an arched trellis extending from one wall to another, thereby zoning the bathroom into two areas while maintaining an open flow of space.

Shelving is also supplied by étagères in painted metal, wood, wicker, and chrome, often narrow enough to put a tiny slice of wall to work and be decorative too.

Placing the bathtub in the center of the room is a popular device that frees wall space to accommodate storage. This Sherle Wagner bathroom has one built-in storage wall that includes a vanity, plus a closet wall, enough space to house just about all of one's personal belongings. Design by Keith Irvine and Thomas Fleming.

FIXTURES, BATH, BASIN BY SHERLE WAGNER INTERNATIONAL

Forget the word "bathroom" and follow your own good sense of taste and style in buying accessories for the bathroom. Choose what you like, what you see anywhere; don't limit yourself to bath shops. Introduce natural materials for a change of pace—in hampers, wastebaskets, accessories. One designer provides the charming idea of hanging assorted straw hats on a bathroom wall. Indulge your fancy for the elegant; put a chandelier over the tub, add gilt fittings, the razzle-dazzle of mirroring, a petite hand-carved marble washbasin.

The floor can be wood or tile, or covered with a synthetic carpet texture for added warmth and insulation. Or it can be marble or slate. And for a touch of class on a floor of mellow wood—the mellowed patterns of a Persian rug.

Face-lifting an Older Bathroom

Designing a new bathroom from scratch or totally gutting and remodeling an old one will produce an interior that may be the last word in streamlined efficiency and aesthetic charm. But what if the budget simply won't allow for a complete overhaul? In that case, some low-cost changes or some inventive decoration can give a dreary bathroom a much needed face-lift. And even without a sunken tub and exquisite cabinetry, such bathroom renewal can effect a look of vintage character and appealing style.

Much can be done, of course, with color and pattern. A dark or shocking-color enamel paint gives new dimension and a special glow to a dated bathroom. So does a jumbo wallpaper pattern, or a wall covering of such high style and sophistication that one would never think of choosing it for bathroom decoration. A pungent color scheme, such as parrot green and white, can be carried through in a medley of patterns —one for the walls, another for the shower curtain, and yet a third at the window.

Explore all the marvelous water-resistant wall coverings, the limitless portfolio of fabric designs, and the extraordinary high-fashion patterns and colors in toweling to come up with a wonderful new look.

Flea-market finds—in furniture, lighting fixtures, and interesting accessories—can be revitalized or used as they are to provide unexpected touches, in addition to illumination or added storage space.

If the budget permits, some minor remodeling can be accomplished —paneling on the walls, the "boxing in" of an old-fashioned tub or sink, a new tile floor, or simply an installation of wall-to-wall carpeting. If paneling is done, some of the paler finishes will achieve a more contemporary look.

WASHBASIN AND FIXTURES BY SHERLE WAGNER INTERNATIONAL

Those little extras make all the difference. A case in point—a Sherle Wagner bathroom with sculpture-like china basin, pewter and china faucets, rosette-shaped door knobs. The generous application of mirror also enhances. Design by Keith Irvine and Thomas Fleming.

The walls of an old-fashioned bathroom might be just the spot for an assortment of collectibles, such as framed memorabilia or assorted country trivia. More on this kind of collection is discussed in our chapter on finishing touches.

Many people actually prefer the quaintly satisfying style of the kind of bathroom grandmother probably had. Imaginative decorating that bypasses the notions of what should and shouldn't go into this room may be all that is needed to bring a run-down bathroom back to life.

A formerly dreary bathroom was given a fabulous face-lift by the addition of new marble-topped sink-cabinet and the application of a lively floral-stripe wall covering. A charming and highly practical idea: valance and café curtains fashioned from floral-border towels. Interior design by Patricia Hart McMillan.

BIRGE WALLCOVERINGS AND DUNDEE MILLS

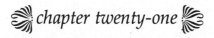

chapter twenty-one

Foyers, Halls, and Stairways

Saving the best for first is an approach not always followed in the decoration of foyers or entry halls. Often an afterthought, these entrance areas are all but ignored, or at best, an obvious expression of where and when the planning and the money ran out.

Treating your foyer this way is like getting all dressed up without combing your hair. This introduction to your home—this opening pronouncement of your decorating preferences and flair, this glimpse into the special life-style of your family—is as important here as in any other area in your home. Possibly more so. Because in one short but very sweet statement, the foyer conveys the message of your home, summing up and predicting at the same time all that is contained within.

Relate Style to Adjacent Areas

As such, the foyer must relate to the decorating style of the living areas beyond, proffering to guests, in capsule form, all the warmth, hospitality, and personal style expressed in those larger rooms. For a visitor, this hospitality is an occasional pleasure; for you and your family, an everyday occurrence. So entrance halls are much more than a special face you put on for the world; they are rooms that greet you as you return, welcoming you warmly back to hearth and home.

Foyers are the last places you leave upon departing, as well. And for this reason they must answer certain practical requirements. There should be a chair or bench for sitting down to put on (or take off) rubbers or overshoes. Some kind of table or cabinet is needed as a receptacle for mail and small packages. A mirror, the bigger the better, permits a quick checkout of appearance on going out and is another must, one that adds enormously to the sparkle as well as spacious feeling of a small entry.

Decorating style and color scheme should relate to any adjacent or open areas, with room for variation on the theme. An accent color in the adjacent dining room, for example, can become the major hue for the foyer. An understated, two-color scheme in the living room becomes lively and exuberant in the foyer, as a third and vivid hue is introduced.

Use Poetic License

The decorating style of the living areas and entry should have consistency, but here, too, there is room for poetic license. If the living room is furnished primarily with modern upholstery, mixed irreverently with a few well-chosen French designs, it might be very effective to dramatize the French elements in foyer decoration.

Rather than a receptacle for recycled attic finds, the foyer can and should be a place in which you can indulge your passion for luxury, even extravagance. For here the quantities are small. Now you can splurge on a gorgeous but expensive wall covering if you need only a few rolls. An oriental rug, which might break the budget in a room-size carpet, is considerably less costly as a small accent.

Go all out on an upholstery pattern if you need only a yard or two for a small bench or slip-seated chair. Own a marvelous but diminutive antique chest? Make it the dramatic focal point of foyer decoration instead of "losing" it within the composition of large-scaled living-room designs.

Need a place to show off a set of framed prints, a collection of Canton ware, a few wonderful etchings? Turn your foyer into a mini-gallery where collectibles can be shown to full advantage, where nothing else competes.

Of course the size and scope of your entrance hall will determine just how much furniture can be used; the amount of available wall space will suggest the possible floor plans. While furniture is occasionally positioned in the center of a foyer, this is feasible only when the area is exceptionally spacious. A round table, even a sculpture on a pedestal, can offer a dramatic centerpiece within a large, square foyer. In a smaller entry, the lack of wall space may preclude the use of any furniture, or at best, one tiny piece. To compensate, a boldly patterned wall covering, a cherished painting, an oversized chandelier can add drama and the necessary enrichment.

If there is room for only a table and one chair, make the table a cabinet instead, to hold gloves, mittens, scarves, and other last-minute "grabs" if no closet is available. Should a closet exist—but the limits of space make you choose between a table and a chair—have both by using a console table, under which can slide a bench or ottoman on casters.

The Dining Foyer

The absence of a dining ell and the presence of a tiny living room may require that all dining take place in the foyer. This must be accomplished skillfully, without diminishing the decorative charm and impact of the entry hall. Possible choices for dining tables are consoles that extend, as well as drop-leaf and flip-top designs, as they economize on space when unopened yet serve adequately even for company meals. For foyer dining, illumination becomes an important consideration. You might install a luminous ceiling or a fabulous chandelier or strategic built-in downlights. Dimmers will help you control the mood, which you will want to change according to the time of day.

Background treatment is especially important for the dining-foyer; it's not very interesting to spend your meal hours staring at a blank wall, no matter how pretty the paint color. Here is the spot to install a handsomely framed mirror or to mirror-sheathe an entire wall. Look into wallpaper murals as a way to create a vista, a sense of scenery or view.

Do whatever you can with the colors, accessories, and flooring you choose to keep this tiny dining area from feeling closed in and uninteresting. If you take many meals in the area, you should provide a practical flooring—ceramic tile, highly waxed wood, vinyl, and even marble. If an accent rug is used, move it out of the way of the table during meal hours. Wall-to-wall carpeting would be a mistake here, unless the cost of frequent cleaning is something with which you can easily live.

The most difficult kind of foyer to decorate is the kind that doesn't exist, a fact of life for many living in a space-shy high-rise apartment. Walking plunk into the living room is not very pleasing to all concerned and it may be essential for you to create a foyer effect with a screen or room divider to establish some kind of vestibule or entry area no matter how small.

If this is impossible, a boldly patterned wall covering, a change of wall paint, or a different floor treatment will visually define an entry even if there is no architectural separation.

Halls and Landings

Similar to the foyer, as a space that serves primarily to lead the way to other areas, the halls and landings of a home should not be decorative stepchildren. Wall and floor treatment is every bit as important in ensuring an allover effect, an integrating decorative statement. In enriching these areas you will avoid the pitfalls of creating deserts and oases—handsomely decorated rooms alternating with drab and arid spaces desperately in need of some kind of embellishment.

Wall-to-wall carpeting, patterned area rugs or orientals, as well as beautiful wood floors, highly polished and refinished as needed (but never slippery), can enhance these halls. Off a kitchen or in a basement area, the flooring can be vinyl or ceramic tile—a material that withstands dirt and is easy to keep clean.

Halls can also be utilized as galleries for photographs, art, collectibles, and so on, in much the same way as an entrance foyer. They may also provide much-needed and usable space for other purposes—possibly for a built-in or free-standing bookcase wall, for a desk, or even a small sitting area. If space permits, a cabinet or dresser can be placed here to catch an overflow of clothing or miscellaneous possessions.

If a hallway has a window, this could become a place for greenery—an upstairs garden area. An abiding favorite for halls is that perennial the grandfather clock, now offered in modern as well as traditional interpretations.

Mirroring, dramatic wall coverings, and excellent illumination are also enhancers for a small or long chamber or back hall. No matter

Masterful overstatement is often called for when a room is large but has no architectural embellishment. In this huge entry hall, the solution was the overscaled beams, added to walls and ceiling and painted stark white. Washable, dark-background floral wall covering, applied to all wall and ceiling surfaces, also helps to create an ingratiating entry.

what their size, hallways and landings will extend the charm of your home if given interesting and imaginative decoration.

Stairways

Decorative interest teams up with safety and practicality for stairway design. The space is a limited one, but the choices are several; careful attention should be paid to the way these stairways are handled.

Skidding is always a danger, so make sure the carpeting you use is skidproof as well as wear-resistant. This is no place for a bargain floor covering; buy the best you can afford in tightly woven, low, or looped-pile texture. You can completely cover up or upholster the stairs, you can run up a narrow width that permits wood to show on either side, or you can simply upholster the treads. For the first option, the labor costs will be steep; the second and third alternatives you can handle yourself.

If the stairs are left bare, give them a nonskid coating that will supply traction. You may need to refinish both the treads and risers if they are badly scuffed.

Decorative treatment should continue the style and color theme of areas into which the stairway feeds and from whence it comes. Some color or colors common to both can be employed as a connecting chain. Walls can be linked by a common pattern or else turned into an interesting gallery of paintings, prints, or family photographs.

Ample lighting is a top priority for stairways, as is a sturdy banister; its absence may require you to put one in. A highly polished banister rim, or one that is color keyed to the wall treatment, can add to the charm of your stairway decoration.

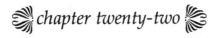

chapter twenty-two

Dens, Libraries, Home Offices, Activity Rooms

Daniel may have walked into the lions' den, but the den in the home, for many years, was off limits to the female of the house. Dark paneling, rugged tweeds, leather, plaids, nautical accessories, hunting trophies, and other for-men-only elements created a domain that belonged primarily to the breadwinner—a place for him to read, work, or relax.

Today, dens, studies, and libraries, the catchall labels for these male-oriented rooms, have all but disappeared from the scene. The high cost of building has turned them into luxuries that few can afford. But rooms set aside for reading or homework, or areas planned especially for this purpose, are flourishing as more and more work is done at home by women as often as by men.

So these new dens or libraries are usually dual-purpose areas, places to install bookcases, to include a desk and file cabinets, as well as some kind of sitting area for private meetings. But they are often reclaimed bedrooms—a fringe benefit of the emptied nest, the vanished sleep-in servant. Sometimes they still have to serve another purpose, as a part-time guest room, an informal living area, a private television or entertainment room-bar.

Special Priorities Come First

Furnishing such a room is not a complicated task, as the special priorities of work space and storage area usually determine what kind of furnishings are to be used. Whatever second or even third role is served by such a room will decide what additional furniture is needed. Available space will set the limits on how much can be purchased and where it will be placed.

We have already discussed, in our chapter on storage, the possibilities of building in shelving and storage, using free-standing designs such as book-stack units, and modular storage and shelving systems. What kind and how much wall space is available, and how large the budget, will be the major factors shaping this choice. Another guideline is permanence. If the home is only a temporary one, it seldom pays to install costly built-ins that cannot be moved with you to the next abode.

Desks and Decoration

Desks or writing tables can be an integrated part of the shelving system or a free-standing design. Many wall-storage collections contain both console table units or fully partitioned desks among the module designs. Establishing an all-encompassing study area, with shelf, cabinet storage, and desk unit contained within one arrangement, is an especially efficient and compact way of handling space. Such a wall can also contain a bar module as well as housing designed specifically for television and stereo equipment. For a larger room, one may have the space for a large and separate desk, as well as a full storage wall. The desk can be positioned out in the room, very much the way it would be placed in an executive's office. This approach frees the walls for more storage area or for some kind of sitting arrangement.

The decoration of today's den-study-home office is no longer limited to leather and tweeds—the masculine stereotype—but these rooms are hardly the places for psychedelic wall-covering patterns and eye-stopping color schemes. Anything distracting is usually undesirable in a room geared to study, work, or reading. The color plan need not be bland to the point of tedium, but it should not be startling or dramatic either. Something in between is called for; the degree of subtlety should be based on your personal needs and tastes.

Good insulation is important, so give preference here to wall-to-wall or room-size carpeting rather than to a smooth flooring material. A completely carpeted floor will add psychological as well as physical warmth, helpful qualities to those laboring over that "best seller" or household bills.

Even in real offices, high up in downtown buildings, the no-nonsense, no frills, all-business look of hard-edged decorating has been softened. Today's executive suites are usually comfortable and home-like sitting rooms, as well as efficient offices, filled with tastefully chosen furnishings and personal accessories.

LEVOLOR LORENTZEN, INC.

Small, well-organized study area permits a writer/author to utilize her bedroom as a home office too. Storage tower, which eats up space vertically rather than horizontally, also creates an alcove for the bed. Striped, narrow venetian blinds, in rich tones of orange and bronze, give a decorative but sleek look at the window. Designer: Scruggs-Myers & Associates.

So while an at-home office should be well organized, and fitted with ample storage and desk facilities, it, too, should offer a relaxed and hospitable warmth. All electrical equipment must be stored out of sight when the room is enjoyed for other purposes. Paneling can and should be used, if a tailored effect is desired, but the finishes can be light and space-giving, not exclusively dark and somber. Sheathing the wall with fabric, such as linen or felt, is another satisfying way of adding warmth, insulation, and a rich backdrop.

To maintain a mood consistent with the role of a den or home office, one should bypass overly elaborate or gussied-up window treatments. Shutters, vertical or Venetian blinds, shades—Roman or laminated— and tailored draperies are among the many possible dressings. Avoiding the fullness of a frilly window style is practical too, as billowy curtains tend to occupy space visually as well as literally.

When more than one person works at home, it is sometimes necessary to set up another study or at-home office area. This might also be the case where there is no separate room that can be zoned off for such a purpose. Establishing an area within the parameters of another room is not that difficult, since there are many rooms in which you can place a writing table or desk, storage or file space, adequate task lighting, a sturdy chair. With a little imagination, and perhaps some juggling of furniture, you might find space in the bedroom, living room, family room, kitchen—even the bathroom.

Budget Savers

Anyone on a tight budget should check out all of the beautifully engineered desk, storage, and upholstered designs now available in K-D (knock-down) collections. Because they save substantially on a sizable amount of labor—since you assemble the furniture yourself—manufacturers of this kind of furniture are able to pass along the financial benefits. If you can read directions and use a screw driver, you can put together handsome furniture at a fraction of what it would cost you to buy it fully assembled. Since so much of this furniture is offered in tailored and casual contemporary styling, it offers a wonderful choice for work-at-home rooms. And as you can take the furniture home with you, since stores stock them in totable cartons, you don't have to wait for months to complete a desperately needed study center.

MALAYA WALLCOVERING FROM THE STILLWATER COLLECTION BY NILS ANDERSON STUDIOS

Steel sawhorses and an oval slab of glass create a small work and study center that also serves as a dining alcove. Strongly patterned, ethnic-inspired wall covering is framed by add-on beams and molding. Wall covering is continued into the living area and is even used behind the bookshelves.

Personal Touches

Don't be afraid of introducing personal accents and touches into your home office; it's an obvious route to making the area more interesting and more individual. A clutch of family photographs on a table or a montage of framed photographs on a wall, the memorabilia of wonderful trips, a collection of your children's artwork or pottery, any mementos or trophies of sporting interests or hobbies can personalize the room. So will baskets of plants if adequate light will nourish their growth.

Whatever style you choose for it, or wherever it is, a study or home office must have sufficient storage, should be a-place-for-everything kind of room. Unless you can control clutter, find everything and enjoy the room with ease, you can't operate at top efficiency.

Activity or Hobby Rooms

In a recent issue, a well-known decorating magazine featured a contemporary version of the American farmhouse, attractively decorated and encompassing the trendy all-in-one living-dining-cooking space. But what really made it newsworthy were the two activity centers—one a first-floor crafts room for a handweaver, the other an upstairs skylight studio for an at-home painter.

This story dramatized a recurring theme of the American life-style today—the preoccupation with hobbies, crafts, and other leisure-time activities. Quite obviously, the family who can devote this many rooms to the enjoyment of their hobby must have ample money, an empty nest, or an only child. For most of us, often living with fewer and smaller rooms, the pursuit of such hobbies puts added pressure on the space budget.

Of course, sometimes an unused bedroom can be converted into a studio, a den, or family room utilized primarily for one or more avocations. But to create an activity center within the home often requires the "discovery" of hidden space—a nook or cranny, an extra closet—whose potential has not yet been realized. The other alternative is to borrow space, to snatch a corner, a wall, even a large area from one of the living, dining, or bedroom parts of the home.

Whatever the case, no active home-hobbyist can function properly unless he or she has some special space set aside for his needs. It must supply whatever work surface is necessary, as well as sufficient storage to organize and house all materials. And if the hobby center is contained within a larger room, its design and color scheme must coordinate with the rest.

Popular hobbies are as many as they are varied—painting, sculpting, sewing, weaving, needlecraft, pottery, gardening, photography, model shipbuilding, rugmaking, and carpentry are some of the favorite ones.

Some hobbies are clean (sewing, weaving, quilting, leatherwork); others, such as painting and photography, involve at least a minimum amount of messing up, so decorating materials chosen must also allow for these factors.

There are many reference books available for the would-be candlemaker and the promising tie-dyer, but very little has been written on how a hobby center should be planned. Most people seem to think that "dirty" hobbies belong in the basement and garage; only the cleaner ones should be practiced upstairs. But with the proper arrangement and choice of furnishings and materials the messier pursuits can be positioned anywhere.

The size of the area is often more difficult to determine, but usually you can judge this in proportion to the amount of equipment needed and the various procedures involved. Sewing, for example, requires fabrics, trimmings, spools of thread, needles, notions, tapes, scissors, and patterns, not to mention counter surface for cutting, basting, and pinning. There must be room to place a dress form, a comfortable work chair, and excellent lighting. Other hobbies, such as candlemaking, require a minimum of materials, tools, and work space, so you can often establish its work center in a small section of an other-purpose room.

Unless a specific kind of table surface is needed—such as a drawing board or easel—you can probably incorporate the counter area within the storage wall of a family room, den, or bedroom. This wall could be custom-built, a home project, or an arrangement of modular storage units, which these days often include fully partitioned activity centers especially designed for sewing, photography, typing, etc. Be sure that whatever counter space you do have is the proper height for the craft; it would be a mistake to compromise on a table that is too high or too low or to make do with a recycled chair that does not provide firm back support.

Specially designed sewing cabinets should feature a pull-up shelf that stores the sewing machine out of sight within a cabinet but is easily accessible. If you do not plan to use such a cabinet, arrange for a permanent place for the machine, no matter how "portable" it is supposed to be.

The same approach holds true for other hobbies. If, you weave, then you must find a stationary place for the loom; for an artist or illustrator, a set position for the drawing board.

Hobbies are so diverse and the requirements are therefore so different that it would take pages to deal effectively with each and every one, which is not the purpose of this book. There are some general principles to be followed, however, that will help you to fashion an area or center that works best for your activity.

Your need for lighting will vary enormously. A painter should enjoy as much natural light as possible; this might even entail installing a skylight, if feasible. The photographer requires a darkroom, so if he cannot take over a separate, and preferably windowless room, he must block out the light with proper screening and set up a darkroom in an unused closet or bathroom if it is possible to utilize one corner of a family room or den for other phases of his work.

The noise factor must be accounted for if the hobby is jewelry-making or carpentry. In these cases, the buffing wheel or power tools will make a racket that should be buffered from the rest of the house. If possible, position these activities in rooms or areas that can be closed off; or invest in an acoustical ceiling and whatever wall covering will aid in muffling the sounds.

Any of the synthetic carpets can provide a warm and handsome base in a family room that contains a sewing center. Bits of fabric and thread can be vacuumed off, although the area near the sewing will tend to mess up faster if it has a carpet below rather than smooth flooring. For some activities, however, a smooth, easily scrubbable floor is *"de rigueur"*—photography, painting, pottery-making, indoor gardening, and dyeing. Certainly this would be the case wherever water or spillable materials (chemicals) are employed.

Judging the amount of storage is tricky; one usually tends to underestimate. It's better to have more than you think you need, especially since you will inevitably be adding to your equipment and raw materials. Don't feel it is necessary to store everything behind cabinet doors. Open shelves are not only acceptable, they are even desirable, as they facilitate finding what is needed. Displaying the materials and finished products on these shelves (skeins of colorful wool), on a cork wall

This cozy sitting room is also a beautifully organized and marvelously equipped activity center, thanks to maple-finished wall units, which store and arrange all the tools and materials of an aspiring needle-worker. Braided rug, country plaids and patchwork, and decorated rocking chair play up the room's unmistakable American charm. Designed by Abbey Darrer.

(photographs), or suspended from the ceiling (model airplanes) will give an activity center its decorative "accents."

Often an interesting craft can really personalize a room when no attempt is made at concealment. An enamelist's setup near the French doors of a bedroom window, spindles of yarn suspended from a pegboard, an embroidery stand in full sight, rows of clay pots and baskets in a converted breezeway-garden room—all will project a unique kind of visual excitement and enrich the character of the life-style within the home.

After furnishing a complement of "necessary" rooms, there is not much money left over, if any, to purchase what is needed for an activity center. If such a center is established within the modular system of a family room, some additional cabinets, a back-supporting chair, and the tools of the trade may be all that is needed. If starting from scratch, however, you might consider a home-constructed center, especially if the hobby is carpentry, or else find secondhand items that can be recycled. Certain activities are harder on furniture than others, so the latter approach is often the most practical even if this entails changing the bases of tables or cabinets to make them even more sturdy.

part four

THE ABCs
OF FINISHING
TOUCHES

Introduction

Decorative accessories are so much more than superficial embellishment. They are the finishing touches, the touches that bring a room to life, that tie it all together, that give it the stamp of a personal taste and life-style. A doubting Thomas need only cover up all of the accessories and wall decoration in any photograph of a beautiful room to discover the truth of this principle. Without these touches, the room is sterile, impersonal, and fragmented, no matter how skillful the furniture arrangement and decorating style, no matter how handsome the furniture, fabrics, and rugs.

There are many ways, as well as places, to add accessories to your rooms—on the walls, on tabletops, on seating designs, on cabinets and other shelved storage pieces, even on beds. How do you go about this, what pieces do you choose, how much is too much? The answer to the first question is "slowly," and if you do this, the rest will follow naturally enough. Your tastes in accents and paintings and pillows should be fairly consistent with your preferences in furniture and fabrics, although sometimes an inspired and unexpected choice can reinforce a specific decorating theme. For an eclectic room with contemporary upholstery, for example, you might want to concentrate on traditional accents, to introduce additional period flavor. A classic English eighteenth-century dining room, on the other hand, might gain a welcome modern accent in the form of an abstract painting.

Where would colorful Americana country rooms be without collections? These often guarantee that fascinating kind of clutter that makes such rooms so endearing.

The decorative game plan of each room will give you ample guidance toward the kind and style of your accessories and wall hangings. As it is never easy to come by what you like—at the right price—the going is often quite slow. This is all to the good. As you start to collect, you will also be formulating arrangements, not merely throwing your accessories around. Our chapter on decorating with all the major kinds of accents follows here, and should give you some helpful guidelines. Of course the initial arrangement must be a fluid one; as you add more pieces you will also be adjusting or even completely revamping the original composition. Eventually you will reach a point of no return that is easy to recognize. The arrangement will be pleasing from many angles; any additional elements will crowd. It is time to stop.

If you are a clutterer, your wardrobe of accents and wall decor will be substantially greater than that of a minimalist, who purposefully creates an almost Spartan-like ambience. Most of us are somewhere in between. Whatever the approach, it is not how much we collect that really matters but the discipline with which we place and arrange our possessions.

And even the most ardent fan of the "more is more" school must leave some kind of breathing space, especially on any tabletop where there is a need to set down a tray of *hors d'oeuvres* or a cup of tea.

You may have assigned a special role to your wall art and room accessories that can give focus and direction to their texture, color, or design. In a setting of subtle neutrals, you may decide to make the accents serve as bright touches of color. In this instance, you would be more likely to choose vibrant pillow patterns, an eye-stopping medley of bibelots, or a collection of brilliantly hued canvases.

Or your accessories can augment the natural, handcrafted style of stripped-pine furniture, homespun fabrics, and handwoven rugs. Macramé wall hangings, informal pillow fabrics, handmade pottery, and Early American baskets will enhance this mood.

As you arrange your accessories, take into account how well they work in concert with other accents, and with the room itself. There's no point, for example, in placing a tall cachepot on a mantel if it partially obscures a painting on the same mantel wall. Or using a vase on an end table that repeats the shape and possibly the texture of the lamp. Search for variation in size, shape, color, and material, unless you are assembling a collection in which one or more of these features will be the common denominator.

Balance is not always equated with symmetry; asymmetrical groupings can also be pleasing and impart a special balance of their own—in relation to other objects or to furniture that is close-by. Accessories can balance one another; a group of porcelain figures or pewter candlesticks on one end of a mantel will balance a framed watercolor hung off center above it. A basket filled with baby's breath can fill in the empty wall space above a cabinet or armoire.

Think also in terms of soft and hard accents. A leafy plant in a basket container blends in satisfying counterpoint to a metal or ceramic box because their textures and shapes are so different.

As you arrange your accessories, and hang your walls, check the effect from more than one vantage point. The look will be different in each case, but the composition must work each time.

Proceed without trepidation; your chances of making costly mistakes are less likely to happen. If a box doesn't work on one table, it may be perfect for another. Arrangements should be arrived at via trial and error, not predetermined with templates and graph paper. It's fun to buy on impulse, to bring home the unanticipated, even the whimsical. After all, there's none of the hassle that you have to go through to move heavy furniture around; accessories weigh comparatively little.

Enjoy the spirit of serendipity as you search for your treasures, as you delight in manipulating them or weaving them into the settings you have designed. Follow the simple guidelines, exercise some restraint, don't buy indiscriminately. Never apologize because you haven't bought that last ashtray. Only a fool or a display expert would decorate that completely and that rapidly. For when it comes to the finishing touches, your home should remain in a state of flux, never frozen into some final, immutable arrangement. As you continue to unearth new finds and fresh discoveries, you will add moments of your present life to the mementos of your past. In this way you will "recharge" your rooms, adding new vigor, welcome changes, a spark that keeps your home interesting and satisfying.

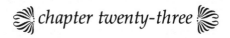

chapter twenty-three

Accessories

Wall Decor

Wall decoration and ornamentation have been prey to the passing whims of fad and fashions in a more obvious way than any other accessory art. Once all but ignored, except by self-motivated art collectors, walls suddenly became a showcase for every kind of decoration imaginable, and a status symbol as those new to the game of acquiring art and graphics found another way of "keeping up with the Joneses."

During the heyday of wall ornamentation, which is less than a few years back, professionals and amateurs alike went to no limits to cover almost every available inch of wall space with some kind of hanging. The wall arrangement or grouping was born, and with it a new kind of collecting mania. Sometimes an entire wall would be covered with paintings, prints, wood carvings, giant letters, and engravings, artfully juxtaposed.

But in recent years, as designers searched for a fresh way of covering almost as much wall space, they zeroed in on oversized paintings, huge graphics, and jumbo posters. A room with one of these maxi-hangings over the sofa, the dining-room server, or on the fireplace wall became the new look, the "in" look. Collections were out, big and single was in, and many artists and poster designers complied happily with the demand for supersized creations.

This new approach, whose life span cannot be anticipated, is a fashion with a redeeming fringe benefit. The formularized wall arrangement, as described above, once *"de rigueur"* for almost every room, is no longer an approach followed so slavishly that many living rooms tend to be look-alikes no matter how different their style. Today there is a freer and more personal use of wall decoration. Sometimes a single painting is used, and occasionally a group of three, and in rooms where it fits, a fascinating arangement of collectibles is used.

Paintings

Paintings and other kinds of wall art should be purchased for their intrinsic value, because you really like them, not because they are the right size—either large enough to stand alone or small enough to work in well with other items. Nor should they be bought because the color ties in perfectly with a room's color scheme—a tasteless and sterile way to embellish walls or to buy art. Paintings can and should introduce fresh colors to a room, a welcome relief to a precisely coordinated color scheme. If some of the colors happen to relate, well and good, but in choosing or ordering custom-created (some designers actually do this) exact-match artwork, you'll be working your color scheme to the point of overkill.

Large paintings are both effective and dramatic, especially when one wants to achieve a clean, contemporary style and use a minimum of wall hangings. But again, these should be chosen because one feels an aesthetic and emotional response, not because "it would look just perfect over the sofa" or because there is some desperate need to fill in empty wall space. Once you buy a painting you really want, no matter what its size, you'll have no trouble finding a place for it.

A single painting can be used alone, on an appropriate slice of wall, or can anchor and focus on an interesting furniture piece. It can be hung over a sofa or a dresser, centered or to one side, or placed above a cabinet or table. If the painting is quite large, hang it low, so that most of it is at eye level; it should not be wider than the table over which it hangs nor less than half its width.

It is also preferable to use single and large paintings in rooms sheathed with patterned wall coverings. Lots of little wall decorations look inconsequential or fight with the design of the wall pattern, generating an unpleasant, "busy" effect. One large painting, graphic, or other wall hanging has more impact.

A narrow slice of wall is dramatized with an artful composition that is extraordinarily simple yet visually pleasing. A large abstract painting is hung low over a waterfall-shaped table of almost the identical width. Then a few accents are added—an apothecary floor lamp, a potted amaryllis, an antique box.

Wall arrangements or groupings also have merit, giving decorative interest to a small foyer, turning a stairway wall or a long hallway into a fascinating gallery, adding unexpected color and a personal touch to a small dining ell, a guest bathroom, a bedroom wall. And as a change of pace to the usual graphics and paintings, try a gallery of photographs—blowups of still lifes—which if properly lit can wake up a dark and neglected part of the house.

Country Style

For the country-cluttered wall, it's usually a case of everything goes. The grouping can be one of old metal trays or enamel washbasins, a wallful of baskets of every shape, size, and texture imaginable. A keeping-room, kitchen-dining-area wall boasts eclectic memorabilia—cooking utensils, an old scale, a telephone booth sign, a candy-bar dispenser, an antique broom. In another such area the wall composition mixes baskets with paintings, utensils, and carving boards. One word about baskets here—they have become the signature of country-style walls, used in a variety of forms or mixed with other elements, a popular and inexpensive way of decorating a wall.

In a remodeled barn, the high walls of the all-in-one living space are decorated with antique farmers' tools—hoes, rakes, shovels, and so on. The long wooden window cornice in a country living room becomes a shelf for a collection of Delft plates and old brass and copper pitchers.

New Ideas to Consider

Many other kinds of things are blossoming as popular wall art. In addition to the much-used groups of baskets, plates, and platters, there is macramé, antique oriental or abstract contemporary rugs, tapestries, old and new posters, wood carvings, fans, kites, even articles of clothing such as scarves and hats or elaborate and exotic jackets or coats found in foreign bazaars.

A collection of mirrors is sometimes used, or stained-glass windowpanes in simple frames. Often a wall hanging serves as a device to dramatize the bed. One designer employs large botanical prints, hung close together, in the place of a headboard; another groups posters and paintings for the same purpose. Quilts also create a popular country-style headboard or wall decoration.

In a cathedral living room, or in the remodeled barn described earlier, the wall collectibles or a group of paintings and graphics can be hung high rather than at eye level to punctuate the lofty architecture of the setting.

Screens are also put into service for wall embellishment. A small screen is hung over a sofa or an interesting cabinet; a many-paneled mirrored or Coramandel screen is placed dramatically behind a sofa.

An oversized, beautifully framed mirror is a fine alternative to the maxi-painting. Such mirrors are now available in a wide choice of frame styles and materials, and in a range of prices. When you want to use a single mirror, choose one larger than you had envisioned; most people tend to pick undersized mirrors, and this defeats the purpose. In addition to being very functional, mirrors are also decorative and space-enhancing. Put one wherever you need extra light and sparkle. Even hang mirror on mirror—such as a marvelously framed period design on a mirrored fireplace breakout.

As with other forms of accessorizing, develop an eye for balance and scale. Hang what you like, and where you think it looks best. Don't bury your walls under an army of collectibles, but don't keep them purposely bare, either, just because that's the thing to do this season. It may not be the next. While relating it to the room as a whole, treat each wall as a self-contained space, and this space includes any piece of furniture placed against it. You may want to create an interesting kind of still life by the way you juxtapose a wall hanging or a collection of hangings in relation to the accessory grouping sitting on a console table.

How to Hang and Frame

Avoid hanging pictures too high or too low; they should be at eye level, although as we mentioned above, you might hang paintings high in a cathedral living room. Arrangements can be planned on an equivalent amount of floor space and then transferred according to the developed "blueprint" of the wall in question. But feel free to change and add to the grouping as you acquire new items or simply want a different look. Changing your wall decor is a fast and effective way of freshening up your rooms. It's a lot easier than moving furniture around. Try to cover the original nail marks or else keep some extra wall paint in reserve for touch-ups.

In selecting frames, whenever needed, purchase styles and materials that suit the formality or informality of the subject matter. Obviously a period portrait or still life would take a different frame than an American primitive or an abstract painting. Frames should enhance paintings and graphics, never dominate them.

If you prefer a more decorative and eclectic look, seek out a variety of frame styles. For uniformity, use matched frames. You can even match up prints of different sizes by matting them and framing them identically.

Individual canvases can be highlighted by the picture lights designed for this purpose. Or a track can be installed on the ceiling, with one or more globes focusing on the painting or grouping. Wall washers and uplights can also be adjusted to dramatize a decorative wall.

Tabletop Accessories

A rich natural resource for self-expression that is virtually untapped in many rooms, the table surface—the tops of tables and cabinets—can be exploited as a splendid showcase for personal taste and style.

Bare, neglected surfaces will make a room sterile and anonymous; haphazardly crowded tabletops can promote a sense of chaos and disorder. Neither extreme is desirable, if the effect is one of happenstance. When there is a method to its madness, a disciplined clutter can evoke a special fascination. Underdecorated tabletops that relate to a minimal design approach can also work—because they were planned that way.

What we are saying is that it doesn't matter which school you belong to—the clean or the cluttered—the way you do it is much more important than what you use. Nothing should be left to chance; accessorize your bare table surfaces the way you would paint an empty canvas. Here you are using three-dimensional objects instead of strokes of color, but the elements of composition, balance, scale, shade, and juxtaposition are basic to both.

The way to accessorize any surface is to choose essentials first, purely decorative elements later. Ashtrays, cigarette boxes, possibly a tea service or a tray of decanters, would be necessary objects for a coffee table, end table, sofa, or console table. A nightstand might require a telephone, clock, radio, ashtray; a dresser might need a perfume tray, assorted brushes, a small catchall basket, etc. Sometimes these top priorities fulfill a special function; in other instances they must be positioned on the designated surface because that's the only place available (such as the tray of decanters in a small living room).

When a desk is a work center, then all of its surface objects usually serve a practical purpose—reference books, a bookstand, blotter, inkstand, jar for pens and pencils. No matter how functional, these pieces can still be artfully arranged to create an interesting still life on the working surface.

The overall decorative style of a room will guide you in the selection of accessory designs, both functional pieces and objects that are purely ornamental. But you do not have to work within a rigid formula. Tabletop elements can introduce a change of pace in the decorating mood, inject a note of welcome eclecticism. Still there must be harmony and a common-sense discipline. It would be foolhardy to place driftwood and antique decoys on the coffee table of a room filled with satins and velvets, just as fragile porcelains and exquisite miniature pillboxes might seem glaringly out of place in a supercasual living room of tailored tweeds and leathers.

Collecting Accessories

How does one accumulate tabletop accessories? Should you study the way professionals do it or collect as the object strikes your fancy? The right approach is probably somewhere in between. If you take the magazine arrangements too seriously, you may end up with a room filled with trendy clichés—in today, out next year. By the same token, you should have some idea of what you are about, what kinds of accessories you should be looking for that will be compatible with your interiors yet express your own taste. This will help you to avoid fads and fashions.

Tabletop accessories encompass a whole world of possibilities, but they do narrow down to some basic types. Baskets are often used, not only because they add character, but because they can also store a myriad of small possessions and useful items, such as cocktail napkins, coasters, extra ashtrays.

Bowls are equally dual-purpose; left empty they are decorative; filled, they can offer fruit, nuts, an arrangement of fresh flowers.

Candlesticks are also used frequently for tabletop arrangements, as they add height to balance out lower elements. Clusters of at least three or more are preferable to a pair, which tend to look skimpy and have little impact when grouped with more massive items.

A stack of books or magazines is also useful; make sure the magazines are up-to-date, and avoid beautifully bound miniature volumes unless you are a collector. This can be a trite touch, a designer's pet cliché. Art books and handsomely illustrated books on architecture, interior design, photography, or any interesting subject can be part of a coffee-table still life that will also entertain your guests.

The recessed shelf behind a sofa becomes the setting for a fascinating "still life," an accessory grouping composed of a framed print, a wall fixture, a decorative box, antlers, candlesticks, a vase with blossoms. Note that wood paneling has been installed on the diagonal to create precise pattern interest.

While framed photographs massed on a table or dresser has become a common *"tour de force"* in recent years, don't let its popularity inhibit you if you love to display family pictures or are an avid frame collector. Such groupings add a great deal of warmth and personality to a room.

Think in terms of mixing materials; textural contrast generates visual excitement. Use a crystal ashtray with an enamel box, brass candlesticks with clay-potted plants.

Sculptures fit easily into tabletop compositions, and these can be commercial copies as well as expensive originals. Everyday objects can be converted into sculpture when mounted on a stand, such as a collection of Early American weather vanes or some beautifully shaped conch shells.

Don't run timid in terms of scale and size; some pieces should be larger, others smaller. Often one unexpectedly big element will project a note of drama, such as a tall wooden deer partnered with a long and low box, a crystal ashtray, a porcelain vase filled with flowers.

The large and square coffee table, a frequent component of conversational seating groups, provides a spacious canvas. Inventively treated, such a surface can display a stack of art books, a vase of flowers, a crystal cube, a ceramic swan, a collection of porcelain eggs, a decanter, and two ashtrays. To make the composition less cluttered, place the ashtrays on top of the books.

Collectibles are natural tabletop elements, especially anything with interesting shape, texture, or color. Even flat collections, such as plates, can form a grouping when propped up on stands. If the table is big enough, the components small enough, as many as two separate collections can be positioned on the same surface. In one interesting room we saw a collection of shell-encrusted boxes grouped with antique perfume bottles clustered on a tray.

Variations on a theme always make for interesting personal touches. Instead of two small ashtrays, try one large, square, and low decorative plate. Or use two candlesticks set within large glass hurricanes. Or carry through a theme of blue and white in a collection of disparate accessories.

Display Your Hobbies

Use your hobbies for tabletop decoration. If you play chess, buy a handsome chess set that can be permanently displayed in a convenient place. Skeins of yarn in a low basket can sit on a dresser or end table. Or proudly group on a cabinet top the pottery your children have made in school or camp.

With accessories in hand, you must then go about the business of composing your tabletop. Put down the necessaries first, then add as much as you think you want. Arrange and rearrange; don't settle for the first impulse. Check from more than one vantage point; a coffee-table grouping should look interesting from the sofa as well as from the doorway—in a different kind of way.

Essentially, table surface decorating is a play-it-by-ear experience, a process of adding and subtracting, of playing musical accessories. If convenience is a factor, such as having a tea service or a tray of decanters and snifters within easy reach, then such a component must be placed close to the sofa so that it is accessible. For smaller tables or cabinets, the space is limited, so the arrangement potential for a specific group of accessories is equally restricted.

Once the arrangement seems almost complete, study it for a while to assess the balance, to discover any glaring holes. If the final composition lacks interest or style, search about for a replacement for one or more expendable items. Don't be afraid of repetition; using two baskets or two or three boxes will create the effect of a collection.

Vases need flowers, but this can be a very costly proposition if followed on a daily basis. A great substitute is potted flowers, which have a longer life, or plants, which can have unlimited staying power if the lighting is adequate.

Don't treat the tabletop as a museum display; it can and should be changed or moved around to include a new acquisition or to show off clay pots of spring bulbs in flower. These can be rotated with dried flowers in a basket or assorted leaves massed in a bowl.

Often it can be fun to concentrate on a single textural theme, such as the natural materials of wood, wicker, shells, rocks, and bamboo. Or to play up the gleam of brass in candlesticks, boxes, bowls, assorted animals, eggs, and even baskets.

The way you juxtapose the various components of the table still life will determine how successful its sense of balance, its decorative charm. Small elements can team up with large ones; careful placement will avoid a lopsided effect, will keep the little items from being "drowned out" by the bigger guys. And the final composition should be in scale to the surface it is placed on or the table itself will look awkward and top-heavy.

The right accessories can help to balance a furniture arrangement. A tall sculpture can visually raise the height of an extremely low coffee table.

Be honest with your own feelings about clutter or restraint, and even if you are a born collector, don't turn your living room into a flea market. Nor is there any reason to apologize because you prefer a few well-chosen and well-placed pieces in preference to a busy look. It's no reflection on your pocketbook, but it does say something about your consistency and the courage to be a little different during a time when colorful clutter is all the rage.

Collect your favorite things, and enjoy them, in full display on all your table surfaces. Rome wasn't built in a day; buy slowly but surely if you want good pieces rather than a lot of cheap ones. They're worth the investment and are easier to sell should you change your mind or your style. In any case, save some of the budget for the tops of your tables. They make everything else look that much better.

Pillows, Quilts, Afghans, Shawls

There is an obvious consistency to the patterns of accessorizing: hard surfaces, such as table or dresser tops, get the hard accents of porcelain objects or crystal lamps, whereas cushiony furniture, such as sofas, love seats, and beds, receive more of the same—the plump of pillows and comforters, the soft pampering of quilts, afghans, and shawls.

Soft accents add to the creature comforts of seating designs; they also enhance their decorative style. Imagine a sofa devoid of pillows. The effect would not only be a Spartan one, it would be cold and impersonal as well, for pillows provide more than a finishing accent— they give a human touch, they guarantee that people live within the room and sit upon the sofa.

Pillows

Pillow shapes tend to be trendy, as designers try to be innovative and pillow manufacturers feel a need each year to add fresh spice to their collections. For a season or more, knife-edged, welted pillows were "in"; then these were supplanted by the squared-off pillows with rounded

Turkish corners and no welts. At one time designers loved to pile sofas and love seats with a pride of assorted mini-pillows in a variety of shapes and fabrics, sometimes patterned, sometimes embellished with tapes and fringes. Today, the bigger the better, and often a huge pillow looms higher than the back of the sofa, thus adding a dramatic accent of color and design.

The change in bed dressing—a complement of coordinated elements replacing the simple bedspread—has also altered and expanded the use of pillows. As discussed in our chapter on bedrooms, linen manufacturers now offer, in enormous variety, a host of matched and color-correlated patterned sheets, comforters, dust ruffles, and pillow shams. When dressed with these, the bed becomes a composition of romantic indulgence but is ready for sleep without removing a single cover. To heighten the sense of luxe, the headboard is heaped with pillows, several sleep-sized and shammed, others that are smaller, in lacy rolls or beribboned fabrics, or in a medley of mini-prints. Often this profusion of pillows obviates the need for a headboard altogether.

Of course pillows are not just extravagant afterthoughts; they also soften and make comfortable the many hard-backed seating designs such as all-wood benches and chairs. Pillows can exist independently, as a special kind of upholstery style, as the family of floor pillows, beanbags, and pillowed ottomans demonstrates.

Novelty pillows, with fanciful decorations or amusing shapes and themes, are offered in easy-to-make home-craft kits and in needlepoint designs. And pillows crafted from patchwork are a popular folk art that flavors many a colorful country room.

Afghans and Shawls

Throwing a quilt over the arm of a sofa, a shawl on the back of a love seat, or an afghan at the foot of a bed are effective touches that further an ambience of comfort and luxury. Frothy shawls impart a subtle texture; the openwork of crocheted afghans warms the spirit with its homespun look.

In today's energy-conscious world, shawls and afghans are much more than pretty and colorful accents. They are much-needed wrap-arounds that help maintain body heat in rooms kept colder than formerly to conserve on fuel. More than that, they are also nourishment for the soul, providing a real sense of nesting, of cozy comfort and warmth.

Quilts

Quilts are especially interesting because they now blossom everywhere—not only on the bed. A modern, all-white apartment, with sisal flooring, canvas fabrics, and contemporary upholstery sports walls that are brilliantly splashed with vibrant Amish quilts—a new kind of wall graphic. Within the large open space of a remodeled barn, quilts are hung as high as the rafters.

Those who freak out on quilts, especially faded, time-worn antiques, use them with abandon—for round or rectangular skirted tables, for pillows, for children's cribs, as tie-back draperies, as a Roman shade, a dining-table accent, even a dust ruffle.

An entire bedroom can be a symphony of patchwork. A folded quilt sits at the foot of the bed atop a quilted coverlet, this teamed with a quilted dust ruffle. Still another quilt hangs over a blanket stand, while two or three grace the walls.

The beauty of quilts is that there are never two the same (unless you copy an old one or make it from a kit) and that age does not stale their infinite variety. The older they are, the more marvelous and the more valuable. Check out a local Americana auction if you want to know the kind of prices these quilts are fetching.

You can make your own quilt for much less, either from a kit or by joining a local quilting bee, an entertaining hobby that revives the social camaraderie of earlier days. For a quilt "look" without all the applique work, you can use stencils to make individual block designs, then piece these together, add padding, and stitch over the stenciling. The effect comes close to the real thing.

A quilt collector can enjoy a stash of assorted quilts by rotating them on walls or furniture. One addict changes her quilt with each season of the year, combining it with the same solid color, tailored canopy, bed draperies, and dust ruffle. Every three months there is a fresh look in her bedroom.

A home-quilter can copy traditional designs or make her own. They can be complicated or quite simple, depending on your skill and your taste. A family of quilters leaves the quilting frame standing in a corner of their living room. The house radiates with all the fruits of their creative labors.

Collectibles

Many and assorted reasons are given for the collection mania. For some it satisfies their acquisitive instincts, for others it's merely a pleasurable hobby or a serious intellectual pursuit. More than a few use it for investment, especially if their collectibles have high market value. City dwellers welcome any excuse to visit country flea markets and fairs. One collector describes it as a primordial need to relate our own lives to the past and to the future.

Collecting begins early in life; children start with trading of baseball cards, marbles, stamps, dolls, model cars, then records and books. As adults, our collections tend to be things for our rooms, favorite things showcased on tabletops, shelves, and cabinets for everyday enjoyment.

Usually we are attracted by one specialty or another—pewter, redware, paperweights, Shaker boxes, shells, colored glass bottles, miniature furniture, weather vanes, ceramic animals. We may collect bits and pieces of identifiable trivia, precious relics of a fascinating era, or a horde of beautiful but assorted bibelots that share the common thread of a precise personal taste.

For the ambitious, and the generously budgeted, collections can run to Imari, Meissen, Staffordshire, Majolica, Canton ware, Chinese export porcelains, pre-Columbian sculpture, art glass, bisque, opaline, Wedgwood, Delft, silver, bronze doré, and all the other rare and costly *objets d'art* that are the great treasures of previous generations and varied cultures.

Anything that exists can be collected, and invariably is, so it is not surprising to see collections of shooting-gallery figures, wagon wheels, advertising memorabilia, driftwood, and street signs, forty-year-old American trivia.

Create Sufficient Storage and Display

Don't let collections run amok, or there will be junk-shop chaos instead of visually pleasing, disciplined clutter. To prevent this, the collectomaniac must provide ample, often ingenious, display space.

Open-shelf cabinets, hutches, étagères, and bookshelf systems are indispensable to a collector. So are curio cabinets, tables with a glass lid and recessed shelf, and plate rails added near the top of walls. And ample wall space for hangable collections is an obvious need.

Sculpture pedestals can serve in various ways, as can bracketed individual shelves, a deep mantel on a fireplace, the ample sills of deeply recessed windows. Cabinet surfaces, such as a dresser or dining-room server, can support a collection, and large collectibles, such as an antique trunk, can substitute for a conventional table. An old-fashioned mail-sorting cabinet or apothecary chest offers a multitude of cubbyholes; antique library steps supply storage, as does a nineteenth-century stove.

Avid collectors often order custom-designed units to store and display their possessions more efficiently and more compactly. Compartmented wall-length units made of plexiglass or mirror are fashioned after store and showroom display cases. Oversized étagères are designed in every wood finish or lacquer color imaginable. Glass or lucite shelves, sporting assorted collectibles can screen windows. Recesses and niches may also be fitted with a series of shelves. Collectibles can alternate with books on a shelf or in a cabinet, and some items, such as buttons and coins, can be mounted, framed, and wall-hung. Walls can also be enhanced by small glass-covered display cases that organize mini-collectibles on shallow shelves.

Collecting is fun; it's enriching and educational, too. Try it, you'll love it. But anticipate your storage needs. Before you go all out on any kind of treasure or trivia, decide where and how you can keep it.

≋ Index ≋